International Labour and Employment Compliance Handbook

www.kluwerlawonline.com

Labour and Employment Compliance in the Republic of Korea

International Bar Association

Labour and Employment Compliance in the Republic of Korea

Ninth Edition

Christopher Mandel
Soojung Lee
Sang Wook Cho
Tae Eun Lee

This publication is part of the International Labour and Employment Compliance Handbook, available on www.kluwerlawonline.com

Editors: Salvador del Rey and Robert J. Mignin
Associate Editor: Juan Bonilla

the global voice of the legal profession

Wolters Kluwer

Published by:
Kluwer Law International B.V.
PO Box 316
2400 AH Alphen aan den Rijn
The Netherlands
E-mail: lrs-sales@wolterskluwer.com
Website: www.wolterskluwer.com/en/solutions/kluwerlawinternational

Sold and distributed by:
Wolters Kluwer Legal & Regulatory U.S.
920 Links Avenue
Landisville, PA 17538
United States of America
E-mail: customer.service@wolterskluwer.com

ISBN 978-94-035-2167-1

e-Book: ISBN 978-94-035-2177-0
web-PDF: ISBN 978-94-035-2187-9

All listed titles are also available on lrus.wolterskluwer.com

1. Argentina: Julio César Stefanoni Zani & Enrique Alfredo Betemps, *Labour and Employment Compliance in Argentina, 11th edition*, 2023 (ISBN 978-94-035-1857-2)
2. Australia: John Tuck, Stephen Price, Rosemary Roach, Jack de Flamingh, Nicholas Ellery & Nick Le Mare, *Labour and Employment Compliance in Australia, 6th edition*, 2021 (ISBN 978-94-035-3914-0)
3. Belgium: Chris Van Olmen, *Labour and Employment Compliance in Belgium, 8th edition*, 2023 (ISBN 978-94-035-2197-8)
4. Brazil: Rodrigo Seizo Takano, Andrea Giamondo Massei & Murilo Caldeira Germiniani, *Labour and Employment Compliance in Brazil, 10th edition*, 2023 (ISBN 978-94-035-1897-8)
5. Canada: Kevin Coon, *Labour and Employment Compliance in Canada, 3rd edition*, 2023 (ISBN 978-90-411-9339-1)
6. Chile: Gerardo Otero A., María Dolores Echeverría F., & Javier Sabido, *Labour and Employment Compliance in Chile, 11th edition*, 2023 (ISBN 978-94-035-1987-6)
7. China: King & Wood Mallesons, *Labour and Employment Compliance in China, 6th edition*, 2021 (ISBN 978-94-035-3894-5)
8. France: Pascale Lagesse, *Labour and Employment Compliance in France, 11th edition*, 2023 (ISBN 978-94-035-2137-4)
9. Germany: Gerlind Wisskirchen & Martin Lützeler, *Labour and Employment Compliance in Germany, 11th edition*, 2023 (ISBN 978-94-035-2347-7)
10. India: Manishi Pathak, *Labour and Employment Compliance in India, 11th edition*, 2023 (ISBN 978-94-035-1927-2)
11. Ireland: Duncan Inverarity & Tríona Sugrue, *Labour and Employment Compliance in Ireland, 10th edition*, 2023 (ISBN 978-94-035-2227-2)
12. Israel: Pnina Broder-Manor & Ilan Winder, *Labour and Employment Compliance in Israel, 10th edition*, 2023 (ISBN 978-94-035-2017-1)
13. Italy: Angelo Zambelli, *Labour and Employment Compliance in Italy, 11th edition*, 2023 (ISBN 978-94-035-1957-9)
14. Japan: Yoshikazu Sugino, *Labour and Employment Compliance in Japan, 11th edition*, 2023 (ISBN 978-94-035-1827-5)
15. Republic of Korea: Sang Wook Cho, Soojung Lee, Christopher Mandel & Tae Eun Lee, *Labour and Employment Compliance in the Republic of Korea, 9th edition*, 2023 (ISBN 978-94-035-2167-1)
16. Mexico: Oscar De La Vega Gómez, *Labour and Employment Compliance in Mexico, 11th edition*, 2023 (ISBN 978-94-035-2377-4)
17. The Netherlands: Els de Wind & Cara Pronk, *Labour and Employment Compliance in the Netherlands, 5th edition*, 2022 (ISBN 978-94-035-1594-6)
18. Poland: Barbara Jóźwik, *Labour and Employment Compliance in Poland, 11th edition*, 2023 (ISBN 978-94-035-2407-8)
19. Russia: Anna-Stefaniya Chepik, *Labour and Employment Compliance in Russia*, 2013 (ISBN 978-90-411-4925-1)

20. Saudi Arabia: Sara Khoja & Sarit Thomas, *Labour and Employment Compliance in Saudi Arabia, 6th edition,* 2023 (ISBN 978-94-035-2107-7)
21. South Africa: Susan Stelzner†, Stuart Harrison, Brian Patterson & Zahida Ebrahim, *Labour and Employment Compliance in South Africa, 11th edition,* 2023 (ISBN 978-94-035-2257-9)
22. Spain: Salvador del Rey & Ana Campos, *Labour and Employment Compliance in Spain, 11th edition*, 2023 (978-94-035-2077-3)
23. Turkey: Elif Nur Çakır Vurgun, Gökhan Akçaalan, Özgür Kızıltan & Zeynep Adıyaman, *Labour and Employment Compliance in Turkey, 9th edition*, 2023 (ISBN 978-94-035-2287-6)
24. United Arab Emirates: Sara Khoja & Sarit Thomas, *Labour and Employment Compliance in the United Arab Emirates, 10th edition*, 2023 (ISBN 978-94-035-2047-6)
25. United Kingdom: Ed Mills, Ailie Murray, Anna West, Gareth Walls & Olivia Boyle, *Labour and Employment Compliance in The United Kingdom, 4th edition*, 2023 (ISBN 978-94-035-2317-0)
26. United States: Andrew J. Boling, Robert J. Mignin, Madeline F. Kelleher & David M. Serwer, *Labour and Employment Compliance in the United States, 8th edition*, 2023 (ISBN 978-94-035-1736-0)

International Bar Association
The Global Voice of the Legal Profession

The International Bar Association (IBA), established in 1947, is the world's leading organization of international legal practitioners, bar associations and law societies. The IBA influences the development of international law reform and shapes the future of the legal profession throughout the world. It has a membership of over 40,000 individual lawyers and almost 200 bar associations and law societies spanning all continents. It has considerable expertise in providing assistance to the global legal community.

Grouped into two divisions – the Legal Practice Division and the Public and Professional Interest Division – the IBA covers all practice areas and professional interests, providing members with access to leading experts and up-to-date information. Through the various committees of the divisions, the IBA enables an interchange of information and views among its members as to laws, practices and professional responsibilities relating to the practice of business law around the globe. Additionally, the IBA's high-quality publications and world-class conferences provide unrivalled professional development and network-building opportunities for international legal practitioners and professional associates.

The IBA's Bar Issues Commission provides an invaluable forum for IBA member organisations to discuss all matters relating to law at an international level.

The IBA's Human Rights Institute (IBAHRI) works across the Association, to promote, protect and enforce human rights under a just rule of law, and to preserve the independence of the judiciary and the legal profession worldwide.

Other institutions established by the IBA include the Southern Africa Litigation Centre and the International Legal Assistance Consortium.

Employment and Industrial Relations Law Committee

The aims of the committee are to develop and exchange knowledge of employment and industrial relations law and practice. Members support each other through the provision of innovative ideas and practical assistance on day-to-day issues. In addition, through its journal and through presentations, conferences, the committee ensures the dissemination of up-to-date law and practice in this highly important business area.

International Bar Association Global Employment Institute

The IBA Global Employment Institute (IBA GEI) was formed in early 2010 for the purpose of developing for multinationals and worldwide institutions a global and strategic approach to the key legal issues in the human resources and human capital fields.

Drawing on the resources and expertise of the IBA membership, the IBA GEI will provide a unique contribution in the field of employment, discrimination and immigration law, on a diverse range of global issues, to private and public organizations throughout the world. The IBA GEI is designed to enhance the management, performance and productivity of these organizations and help achieve best practice in their human capital and management functions from a strategic perspective.

The IBA GEI will become the leading voice and authority on global HR issues by virtue of having a number of the world's leading labour and employment practitioners in its ranks, and the support and resource of the world's largest association of international lawyers.

Further information

International Bar Association, 4th Floor, 10 St Bride Street, London EC4A 4AD, United Kingdom, Tel: +44 (0)20 7842 0090, Fax: +44 (0)20 7842 0091, E-mail: member@int-bar.org, www.ibanet.org

About the International Labour and Employment Compliance Handbook

From 1976 through 1988, the International Bar Association and Kluwer Law International published the groundbreaking International Handbook on Contracts of Employment. This Handbook provided one of the first global overviews of the law of the international employment relationship.

Since publishing the first edition, globalization of business has created an increased demand for knowledge of labor and employment laws throughout the world. Therefore, along with Kluwer, we decided to publish an updated Handbook which we have titled the International Labour and Employment Compliance Handbook.

This new Handbook was intended to be a practical guide by providing a general overview of key labor and employment issues in multiple jurisdictions. Each chapter was written so that it is easy to understand by lawyers and non-lawyers alike. Each country author has also followed a standard outline to assist readers in analysing employment issues in each country.

The first edition of this new Handbook included nineteen (19) different countries.

This Handbook would not have been possible without the help and assistance of many people. Most importantly, the individual country authors are all distinguished legal practitioners who spent considerable time drafting and revising their country reports to meet difficult deadlines. We thank each of them. Our friends at Kluwer, especially Ewa Szkatula, have done a wonderful job in keeping the editors and the authors on schedule. Finally, we want to also express our gratitude to Cuatrecasas, Gonçalves Pereira, and Baker & McKenzie LLP for their valuable assistance in the coordination and organization of this project. Our warmest thanks to each of them.

Because of the success of the Handbook, Wolters Kluwer Law & Business decided to publish each country report also as a separate book to give a choice in obtaining the information. We hope this new format will be a helpful and useful resource just like the Handbook. Both formats are available in print and online.

The Editors

Salvador del Rey Guanter
Robert J. Mignin

March 2013

Table of Contents

Republic of Korea

AUTHORS

Sang Wook Cho

Sang Wook Cho is a partner at Yulchon, where he has practised law for over twenty years and currently serves as the chair of its Labor and Employment Practice. Mr Cho advises numerous leading domestic companies as well as foreign businesses, including major multinationals, with respect to all manner of employment and labour issues, including disciplinary actions and dismissals; collective bargaining and workplace organizing; issues relating to part-time and fixed-term employees, and temporary dispatched workers; discrimination and harassment; and large-scale redundancies.

Mr Cho is also deeply involved in Yulchon's labour and employment litigation practice, where he is an integral part of Yulchon's team responsible for formulating the most effective responses by employers to all manner of employee and workforce claims.

Mr Cho is frequently listed as a leading practitioner in the field of Korean employment law by international legal publications, including *Chambers Asia-Pacific* and *Legal 500*. He received his LLB from Seoul National University in 1994, graduated from the Judicial Research and Training Institute of the Supreme Court of Korea, South Korea, in 1998, and received his LLM from Cornell University School of Law, New York, in 2004. He is licensed to practise in the Republic of Korea and speaks both Korean and English.

ADDRESS
Yulchon LLC
Parnas Tower, 38F
521 Teheran-ro, Gangnam-gu

Seoul 06164
Korea
Tel.: +82-2-528-5355
E-mail: swcho@yulchon.com
Web: http://www.yulchon.com

Soojung Lee

Soojung Lee is a senior foreign attorney in Yulchon's Labor and Employment Practice and currently serves as the co-vice chair and head of international employment in its Labor and Employment Practice. Ms Lee advises both domestic and foreign multinational companies in relation to all manner of labour and employment matters in Korea, including workforce reductions, employee and executive terminations, collective labour relations, discrimination, use of non-regular workers, and general employment-law compliance. A native Korean speaker, Ms Lee has extensive experience in both the Korean and US legal and business markets.

Ms Lee has been recognized as a legal expert in the labour and employment field in Korea by prestigious international and domestic publications and directories, such as *Chambers Asia-Pacific* and *Who's Who Legal*. She is a graduate of Yonsei University, Seoul, and Loyola Law School in Los Angeles, where she was a member of the St Thomas More Society and an Article Editor of the *Loyola of Los Angeles Law Review*. Before joining Yulchon LLC, Ms Lee practised law in the Los Angeles office of Sonnenschein Nath & Rosenthal LLP. She also gained public-sector experience while working at the Constitutional Court of Korea as an aide to the Secretary General.

ADDRESS
Yulchon LLC
Parnas Tower, 38F
521 Teheran-ro, Gangnam-gu
Seoul 06164
Korea
Tel.: +82-2-528-5246
E-mail: slee@yulchon.com
Web: http://www.yulchon.com

Christopher Mandel

Christopher Mandel is a New York licensed senior foreign attorney at Yulchon. Mr Mandel graduated *magna cum laude* from the University of Pennsylvania Law School and worked as an associate in the New York office of Sullivan & Cromwell LLP, focusing primarily on mergers and acquisitions and securities matters. He clerked for the Honourable William

H. Yohn, Jr of the United States District Court for the Eastern District of Pennsylvania.

ADDRESS
Yulchon LLC
Parnas Tower, 38F
521 Teheran-ro, Gangnam-gu
Seoul 06164
Korea
Tel.: +82-2-528-5040
E-mail: cmandel@yulchon.com
Web: http://www.yulchon.com

Tae Eun Lee

Tae Eun Lee is a partner at Yulchon. Mr Lee graduated from Seoul National University (LLB) and Sogang University School of Law (JD), South Korea, and completed a visiting scholar programme at Columbia Law School, New York. Mr Lee worked as a visiting international attorney in the New York and Los Angeles offices of Littler Mendelson P.C. He is licensed to practice in Korea and California.

ADDRESS
Yulchon LLC
Parnas Tower, 38F
521 Teheran-ro, Gangnam-gu
Seoul 06164
Korea
Tel.: +82-2-528-5067
E-mail: telee@yulchon.com
Web: http://www.yulchon.com

Legal Compliance in Republic of Korea

1. LEGAL FRAMEWORK: EMPLOYMENT LAWS

1.1. Sources of Employment Law

The sources of employment laws in Korea consist of the Constitution, the Labor Standards Act (LSA), the Trade Union and Labor Relations Adjustment Act (TULRAA), and a variety of other labour and employment-related acts, as well as generally applicable civil and criminal law. The Korean Constitution provides all citizens with a right and a duty to work, and it charges the state with the responsibility for promoting employment and imposing a minimum wage and implementing special protections for women and children in the workforce.[1] The Constitution also guarantees the right to collective bargaining and collective action for private-sector employees.[2]

1.2. Labor Standards Act

The LSA is the primary statute governing an employment relationship, and it regulates the minimum working conditions for employees in individual labour relations between employers and employees. The LSA applies to all workplaces in Korea, but many of the LSA's provisions are not applicable to employers with fewer than five employees.[3] The LSA sets the minimum standards for appropriate working conditions. Any employment agreement

1. Constitution Art. 32.
2. Constitution Art. 33.
3. LSA Art. 11. The LSA, and certain other Korean labour-related statutes – for example, the Minimum Wage Act – also exempt employers who only employ relatives living together, as well as the employment of household/domestic employees, from coverage.

or policies which fall below the minimum standards of the LSA are deemed null and void to such extent.

1.3. Trade Union and Labor Relations Adjustment Act

The TULRAA governs collective labour relations between trade unions and employers. The guaranteed rights of employees with respect to association, collective bargaining and collective action pursuant to Article 33 of the Constitution are codified in the TULRAA.

1.4. Other Employment Laws

In addition to the LSA and the TULRAA, there are other statutes that govern individual employee-employer relations and collective labour relations. The Minimum Wage Act (MWA) establishes the minimum wages that employers must pay to employees. The Protection of Fixed-Term and Part-Time Employees Act (FTPTA) and the Protection of Dispatched Workers Act (DWA) extend various employee protections to fixed-term, part-time, and temporary dispatched workers. The Employee Retirement Benefits Security Act (ERBSA) imposes minimum standards for retirement or severance pay. The Equal Employment and Support for Work-Family Reconciliation Act (EEA), the Prohibition of Age Discrimination in Employment and Aged Employment Promotion Act (AEPA), and the Anti-Discrimination Against and Remedies for Persons with Disabilities Act (PDA) ban employment discrimination on the basis of gender, age, or disability, respectively, and institute policies designed to foster the employment of women, the aged, and people with disabilities.

2. CONTRACTS OF EMPLOYMENT

2.1. Overview

The formation and enforcement of contractual rights and obligations are generally governed by the Korean Civil Act (the 'Civil Act'). However, the LSA is the primary source of legal rules governing an employment relationship. The LSA provides numerous minimum standards to which the terms of an employment relationship must conform, default rules that apply in the absence of a contrary contractual agreement, and other obligations imposed on employers. Its provisions apply to virtually all businesses or workplaces that ordinarily employ five or more employees and some of its provisions apply even to employers with fewer than five employees.

In addition to the statutory provisions that govern employment relationships, such relationships may also, in accordance with the TULRAA, be governed by the terms of a collective bargaining agreement (CBA). An employer's rules of employment (also referred to as 'work rules') – to the extent that they do not conflict with any statutory requirement or valid CBA – may also legally bind employer and employee. All employers who regularly employ ten or more employees in a business or workplace must prepare written work rules and file them with the Ministry of Employment and Labor (MOEL).

Contractual agreements with individual employees may provide additional terms and conditions of employment to the extent that they do not conflict with any statute, CBA, or employer work rules.

2.2. Written Employment Contracts

There is no general rule, under the Civil Act, requiring a writing for the formation of a contract. Nor does the LSA require a writing to form an employment contract, except that part-time employees are required to be provided with a written employment contract. Thus, an employment relationship may be formed by oral agreement. Employment relationships may also, in some circumstances, be formed by operation of law without any agreement.

However, all employers are required to provide each employee with at least a written statement of certain primary employment terms, or any changes thereto.[4] These terms include wages, working and rest hours, days off, and annual leave. With respect to fixed-term employees, these terms also include the contract period, the place of employment, and the nature of the work. For part-time employees, the work days and working hours for each day must also be stated in writing.

For regular (permanent) employees, the employer must only 'clearly state' (though not necessarily in writing) the place of employment and work to be performed. The employer must also 'clearly state' to all employees, whether full-time or part-time, the other matters required to be included in the work rules of an employer with ten or more employees (pursuant to the LSA).

In practice, all of these terms are generally stated through a combination of a written employment contract or letter, and the company's work rules.

4. LSA Art. 17.

Failure to provide the required statement of employment terms is an offence punishable by a fine of up to South Korean Won (KRW) 5 million.[5]

A liquidated damages clause in an employment contract is unenforceable.[6]

2.3. Oral Contracts

Although legally permissible, it is not advisable to orally enter into an employment contract given the inherent difficulty of conclusively establishing its terms and the requirement that certain employment terms should be stated in writing, as explained above in section 2.2. Moreover, in the absence of a written contract limiting an employee to a fixed term, an employment relationship is generally of indefinite duration by default. Written employment agreements should also explicitly state that they may be amended only in writing to avoid potential disputes over purported orally agreed changes to terms of employment.

2.4. Employee Handbooks (Work Rules)

Employers that ordinarily employ ten or more people must prepare written work rules concerning certain enumerated subjects.[7] The subjects that must be addressed are matters pertaining to the following (although certain of these items are allowed to be omitted if they are not relevant):

(i) Starting and finishing times, recess hours, days off, leave, and shifts.
(ii) Determination of wages, calculation of wages, means of payment, payment intervals, time of payment, and wage increases.
(iii) Calculation of family allowances and means of payment.
(iv) Retirement.
(v) Retirement/severance benefits required by the ERBSA, bonuses, and minimum wages.
(vi) Meal allowances and the allocation of expenses for operational tools or necessities.
(vii) Educational facilities for workers.
(viii) Maternity protections for female workers, such as maternity leave and childcare leave, and support for reconciliation between work and family life.

5. LSA Arts 17 & 114, FTPTA Arts 17 & 24(2).
6. LSA Art. 20.
7. LSA Art. 93.

(ix) Safety and health.
(x) Improvement of workplace environments according to employees' characteristics, such as gender, age, or physical attributes.
(xi) Support with respect to occupational or non-occupational accidents.
(xii) Prevention of workplace harassment and measures to take when workplace harassment occurs.[8]
(xiii) Award and punishment.
(xiv) Other matters applicable to all employees of the business concerned.

The requirement that an employer's work rules address a given subject is not a requirement that an employer provide the relevant subject matter itself.

These work rules may be contained in an 'employee handbook', or in a collection of policy documents on various individual topics. They are binding and can override any terms in an individual employment contract that are less favourable to employees.

Even employers with fewer than ten employees may have 'work rules' to the extent that they apply rules (including unwritten rules) or practices that govern the fundamental terms and conditions of employment. The work rules of such employers need not cover all the matters listed above, nor are they required to be filed with the MOEL. However, these work rules may still be legally binding. And for employers with five or more employees, they are subject to mandatory employee consultation and consent requirements like those discussed immediately below with respect to formally prepared and filed work rules.

In order to prepare and amend its work rules, an employer that ordinarily employs five or more employees must consult with either: (i) a union representing more than 50% of the employees in the business or affected workplace; or (ii) if no such union exists, a majority of those employees.[9] To amend the rules of employment to the detriment of employees, the collective consent of a majority of employees is required.[10] Once prepared in accordance with these requirements, the new or amended work rules must be filed with the MOEL. The filing must include evidence of the employee consultation. If an employer adversely amends its work rules without satisfying the consultation and consent requirements, the change is effective with respect to the employees who are hired in the future but is ineffective

8. The requirement to address non-sexual workplace harassment was added by an amendment to the LSA, effective 16 Jul. 2019.
9. LSA Art. 94.
10. There is a narrow judicially crafted exception to this majority-consent rule, where the change is 'reasonable in light of socially accepted norms'. This is reserved for very limited circumstances.

as to the current employees. Instituting or amending work rules without complying with these consultation, consent, and reporting requirements is punishable by a fine of up to KRW 5 million.[11]

2.5. Job Descriptions

See sections 2.2 and 3.2.

2.6. Offer Letters

An offer letter may be used as a preliminary statement of expected terms of employment, with the definitive terms subsequently set forth in a more comprehensive employment agreement, so long as the offer letter is clear that it does not constitute a final employment contract. In cases where an employer has comprehensive work rules in place, a simple offer letter with only the specific terms applicable to the relevant individual employee may also suffice in lieu of a more comprehensive employment contract, so long as the employer makes clear that the prospective employee will be subject to the employer's work rules, and those rules are provided to that individual.

2.7. Checklist of Do's and Don'ts

- Institute a simple set of work rules that satisfy the statutory requirements, ideally before hiring more than four employees.
- If an existing operation has no work rules, they should be prepared so as to formally codify existing practice – with modifications if desired – and majority consent should be sought from the employees to avoid potential disputes over claimed disadvantageous changes.
- Have a standard employment agreement (or letter) prepared that covers all matters statutorily required to be clearly stated to employees in writing, namely: wages, working hours, days off, and annual leave. Place of employment, and work to be performed, can be included in the agreement or otherwise clearly stated for indefinite-term employees. The agreement should also make clear that the employer's work rules apply to the employee, and those rules should be provided to the employee.
- Bear in mind that a liquidated damages clause in an employment contract is void.

11. LSA Arts 94 & 114.

3. RECRUITING, INTERVIEWING, SCREENING AND HIRING EMPLOYEES

3.1. Overview

The LSA is the primary law governing the mandatory and permissible terms of an employment relationship, but it has little to say about how an employer must treat a *prospective* employee. Various other statutes, however, impose a variety of rules on the hiring process, most importantly: (i) prohibitions on various forms of discrimination (*see* section 15); (ii) legal protections for the personal information of prospective employees, as well as employees (*see* section 16); and (iii) special obligations with respect to the employment of foreign workers (*see* section 13).

3.2. Recruiting

The Fair Hiring Procedure Act (FHPA) imposes a number of prohibitions and obligations on certain employers with respect to their hiring practices. The FHPA applied to employers with at least three hundred employees as of 1 January 2015, and as of 1 January 2017, it has expanded to cover all employers with thirty or more employees.

The FHPA prohibits false or deceptive job advertisements by covered employers and imposes criminal penalties of up to five years of imprisonment or a KRW 20 million fine for violating this prohibition.[12] The FHPA also mandates that covered employers should not unfavourably change the terms and conditions stated in the job advertisement after hiring, and upon an applicant's request, a covered employer must return any documentation submitted by the applicant. Violation of these requirements may result in a fine of up to KRW 5 million.[13]

Indicative of a commitment to anti-corruption in recruiting, the National Assembly amended the FHPA in 2019 to (i) prohibit certain corrupt hiring practices, such as lobbying and offering gifts;[14] and (ii) prohibit employers from requesting personal information such as an applicant's physical appearance and hometown, unrelated to the job requirements or the applicant's merit.[15] Although the language of the amended FHPA could be interpreted otherwise, and there appear to be no court decisions interpreting the amended law yet, given the legislative history, it appears likely that requesting an applicant's ID-style photograph – a common feature in Korean

12. FHPA Arts 4 & 16.
13. FHPA Arts 4 & 17.
14. FHPA Arts 4-2 & 17.
15. FHPA Arts 4-3 & 17.

job applications – will still be permissible. These amendments became effective on 17 July 2019 and impose a fine for violating these new prohibitions of up to KRW 30 million for violating (i) and up to KRW 5 million for violating (ii).

For employers not covered by the FHPA, there are no other salient specific procedural requirements for the recruitment of employees, except those required as to certain non-exempt foreign employees (*see* section 13.2). Instead, employers must avoid unlawful discriminatory practices in their recruitment procedure (*see* section 15); obtain any consent required for the collection of personal information from applicants, and otherwise comply with all applicable privacy laws (*see* section 16); and ensure that they do not hire a non-Korean who is not authorized to work in Korea (*see* section 13).

Typically, potential applicants are invited to submit their resumes and other requested documentation of education and experience, and selected applicants are invited to attend an interview, after which an offer or offers may be extended. Potential pitfalls in this process are discussed in more detail below.

The recruitment of foreign workers is subject to specific requirements discussed in section 13.

3.3. Employment Applications

An employment application form should avoid any enquiries or statements that could be construed as suggesting discriminatory practices, as discussed below, and should obtain consent to the collection and use of an applicant's protected personal information as described in more detail in section 16.

3.4. Pre-employment Enquiries

As a general matter, enquiries that relate to an applicant's educational background, work experience, and job-related skills are entirely permissible in the course of the recruiting process, as is the collection of information necessary to determine an applicant's right to work in Korea, such as the individual's national or foreign registration number. Enquiries that could give rise to an appearance of unlawful discrimination, such as enquiries about an applicant's marital status, children, pregnancy or plans to become pregnant, physical appearance, physical disability, or past union activities, should be avoided or, where genuinely necessary in light of the nature of the job, treated with great caution.

After an offer of employment has been extended, an employer may more freely enquire about matters such as an applicant's need for reasonable accommodation for a disability, marital status, and children (for purposes of tax adjustment and any family-related benefits).

3.5. Pre-employment Tests and Examinations

Employers are specifically prohibited from utilizing any test or examination to ascertain whether a job applicant is disabled unless the test is required in light of the nature of the relevant job duties.[16]

Additionally, the use of pre-employment tests that are not clearly job-related may expose an employer to legal risk for discrimination claims. This risk is enhanced by the fact that 'disparate-impact' may be argued in many kinds of discrimination claims (e.g., age, gender, and disability) with respect to ostensibly neutral practices.

After having received an offer of employment, an individual may be asked to submit to standard medical testing. Employers are required to avoid the use of employees with contagious diseases or mental illnesses, or any other disease that could worsen due to their work, for which testing may be a legitimate necessity.

3.6. Background, Reference and Credit Checks

In general, any background, reference, or credit check of a job applicant, will involve obtaining legally protected personal information about the applicant from third parties. Obtaining legally protected personal information about the applicant will require consent if the information is not 'necessary' to enter into an employment relationship with the applicant, and obtaining any personal information about the applicant from a third party will at least require that the applicant be notified of the source, purpose, and right to demand suspension of processing, either at the applicant's request or if the employer processes a significant amount of personal information (set by regulation). *See* section 16 for a more detailed discussion of these requirements.

A credit check, in particular, is also governed by the Use and Protection of Credit Information Act (the 'Credit Report Act'), which requires that an employer or other person obtain consent from an individual in order to obtain their credit report, including specific consent to its use for employment purposes.[17]

Additionally, obtaining detailed and frank reference information from prior employers may be practically difficult in Korea, because in addition to

16. PDA Art. 12(1).
17. Credit Report Act Arts 32(2) & 33.

the consent requirement under the personal information protection law, Korean defamation law is very strict and can result in criminal sanctions, and truth is not an absolute defence to a defamation claim. The LSA also prohibits employers from communicating for the purpose of interfering with a worker's employment.[18]

3.7. Fines and Penalties

Penalties under the FHPA are discussed above. The penalties – including fines and, in some cases, imprisonment – that can be imposed for engaging in discriminatory conduct in the hiring process depend on the nature of the discriminatory conduct and are discussed in more detail in section 15. The penalties for violating laws relating to the privacy of applicants' personal information are discussed in more detail in section 16.

Additionally, where a person violates provisions of Korean labour law such that a criminal penalty is imposed, any relevant criminal fine generally may be imposed on the employer as well unless the employer exercised appropriate supervision so as to avoid the violation.

3.8. Checklist of Do's and Don'ts

- Obtain necessary consent for the collection of personal information, including credit information, from job applicants and from third parties.
- Consider whether any pre-employment tests or enquiries are sufficiently related to the relevant job duties. Avoid enquiries or tests that may be construed as impermissibly discriminatory.

4. MANAGING PERFORMANCE/CONDUCT

4.1. Overview

Article 23 of the LSA prohibits an employer that ordinarily employs five or more employees from dismissing,[19] suspending, or transferring an employee, reducing an employee's wages, or taking any other punitive measures against an employee, without 'just cause'. 'Just cause' is not defined in the LSA (except with respect to redundancies, in Article 24 of the LSA, discussed below in section 6). Thus the Korean courts have developed

18. LSA Art. 40.
19. Involuntary dismissal for performance or conduct-related reasons is addressed in s. 5.

the standard through precedent and generally apply the concept strictly so as to fulfil the LSA's purpose of protecting employees.

4.2. Coaching and Counselling

If coaching or counselling is offered to an employee on a voluntary basis, no legal justification is required. However, if an employer wishes to require an employee to accept coaching and counselling in order to improve the employee's performance, such a requirement could potentially be resisted on two grounds: (i) that the required participation itself is a disciplinary measure that requires just cause; or (ii) that the required participation is not within the scope of the employee's duties or the reasonable instructions of the employer, and can be refused without giving rise to any just cause for discipline.

Neither argument is likely to be successful if any coaching or counselling is designed to help improve the employee's performance and does not appear punitive in nature. An employer is, in fact, required to take measures aimed at helping a poorly performing employee to improve before taking any serious disciplinary measures against the employee, and an employee is expected to accept such help. Clearly establishing the basis for evaluating the employee's performance as requiring improvement, through written records, is also advisable. As a best practice, the employer's work rules should contemplate providing mandatory training or requiring that poorly performing employees make efforts to improve.

4.3. Written Evaluations

Regular written evaluations are not uncommon among Korean employers and can be very useful for establishing the basis for any future disciplinary action. Because it is always the employer's burden to show 'just cause' in any proceeding challenging any adverse employment action, and because only a pattern of persistent uncorrected poor performance, or significant misconduct, can provide 'just cause' for severe disciplinary measures, written evaluations can be a useful way of creating a written performance record.

4.4. Types of Discipline: Warnings, Pay Cuts and Suspensions

The most common forms of disciplinary action utilized by Korean employers are warnings (reprimands); pay cuts; and suspensions without pay. Demotions, transfers, and in the most extreme cases, terminations (discussed in section 5) are also utilized as disciplinary measures.

A reprimand is the least severe form of disciplinary action. It generally involves a written notice of misconduct or deficient performance being delivered to the employee, and the employee may also be required to submit a written explanation.

A pay cut is a more severe form of discipline, but the extent of the cut is limited by the LSA to no more than half of one day's *average wages*,[20] per infraction, and no more than one-tenth of the total wages paid during each pay period.[21]

Suspension without pay is yet more severe. It is generally reserved for significant misconduct that may yet fall short of that required for termination.

In all cases where disciplinary measures are applied, they are required to be used fairly and in proportion to the culpability of the relevant employee. Excessively severe disciplinary action that is disproportionate to the deficiency of the employee's conduct will be found to lack just cause if challenged. The justification for discipline should include fair and objective standards; for example, applying discipline solely on the basis of employees' comparative performance (such as the lowest 5% of employees by sales) would be considered unjust.

The scope of available disciplinary measures and the reasons for which they may be used are also generally expected to be clearly stated in an employer's work rules. Attempting to discipline an employee in a manner not clearly contemplated by the employer's work rules is more likely to be found, by a court or the Labor Relations Commission, to lack just cause, except in cases of clear and egregious misconduct. For this reason, even employers that are not required to prepare written work rules because they employ fewer than ten employees may find it advisable to prepare such rules regardless, rather than relying solely on a future tribunal's sense of fairness.

There is no statutory requirement that an employer follow any particular minimum procedure (such as review by a disciplinary action committee) for imposing disciplinary action. However, should the employer's work rules or the relevant CBA require a certain procedure, failure to satisfy such procedural requirement would be a significant defect which might render the action null and void.

If an employee successfully challenges a disciplinary measure before the Labor Relations Commission or in court, the employee is generally entitled

20. 'Average wages' is defined in the LSA, and normally means the prior three months' wages, divided by the total number of days during those three months. Or, if the employee's ordinary wage is higher, the ordinary wage is used in lieu of the average wage. LSA Art. 2(1)(6), (2).
21. LSA Art. 95.

to be paid any lost or reduced compensation and to the reversal of any continuing adverse employment action.

4.5. Checklist of Do's and Don'ts

- Prepare written work rules that clearly describe the performance and conduct standards expected of employees and fair disciplinary measures that may be applied to an employee who violates those standards.
- Keep detailed written records of any performance and conduct issues. Regular employee evaluations are a useful tool and should ideally include objective measures of employee performance, rather than solely subjective impressions, as well as opinions from multiple evaluators. It is always an employer's burden to prove 'just cause' if an adverse employment action is challenged by the affected employee.
- Notify employees of any performance and conduct issues, and offer reasonable advice and opportunities to improve. Do not allow conduct and performance issues to simply go unaddressed.
- Approach disciplinary and performance matters progressively, from less severe to more severe measures, as befits the level of misconduct or poor performance. Employers should only resort to severe disciplinary measures in response to significant misconduct or after persistent failure to respond to lesser measures and to efforts to help the employee improve.

5. TERMINATION OF EMPLOYEES FOR PERFORMANCE OR DISCIPLINARY REASONS

5.1. Overview

'At-will' employment is a rare exception to the norm in Korea. Instead, an employer that ordinarily employs five or more employees must have 'just cause' to terminate any employee before retirement age or before the end of a fixed-term contract period (which generally can be up to two years, as discussed in section 7.2).[22] As discussed in section 4, all disciplinary measures require 'just cause' under LSA Article 23. However, termination is the most severe form of permissible disciplinary action, and as such the standard for 'just cause' is at its strictest in the context of an involuntary dismissal.

'Just cause' for termination is a very exacting standard that can be difficult for employers to satisfy, and as a result, it affords employees robust job protection. Application of the standard varies depending on whether the

22. LSA Arts 11(1)–(2) & 23(1), LSA Enforcement Decree Art. 7 & Table 1.

termination is for reasons related to an individual employee's conduct, or for general business reasons such as restructuring.

In the context of termination for individual performance or disciplinary reasons, 'just cause' requires that some 'fault attributable to the employee' makes continued employment untenable. Examples of conduct that can exhibit the requisite degree of fault include:

(i) grave misconduct that makes it impossible to continue the relationship;
(ii) continuous and persistent unsatisfactory performance, despite efforts to help the employee improve;[23]
(iii) criminal or deliberate tortious acts against the employer;
(iv) serious criminal acts, even outside the scope of employment;
(v) improper relationships with other employees; and
(vi) material misrepresentation in the hiring process.

Whether an employee is dismissed for individual or business reasons, an employer that ordinarily employs five or more employees must provide the terminated employee with written notification of the reasons for the dismissal and the effective date.[24] The dismissal is not effective until this notice is given.

5.2. Separation/Severance Pay

All terminated employees, whether dismissed because of their individual fault or for business reasons, are entitled to thirty days' notice of termination or thirty days' 'ordinary wage' in lieu of notice.[25] 'Ordinary wage' is a legal construct used to calculate various statutory benefits, and it includes all regular, fixed and pre-determinable compensation that is paid uniformly to all employees or to a class of employees.[26] There are limited exceptions to

23. The Supreme Court has held: 'For the dismissal of an employee due to poor work performance to be justified, the employee's work performance should fall below "such a degree at which the employment cannot be continued" under existing social norms, with the employee's work ability not only being "relatively low compared to other workers" but also worse than the "normally expected minimum" for a considerable period of time, with limited possibility of improvement, and while work performance is carefully evaluated based on fair and objective standards.' S. Ct. Case No. 2018Da253680 (21 Feb. 2021).
24. LSA Art. 27, LSA Enforcement Decree Art. 7 & Table 1.
25. LSA Art. 26.
26. *See* S. Ct. Case No. 2012Da89399 (en banc decision), pp. 7–11 (12 Dec. 2013). In this case, the Supreme Court resolved a long-standing dispute over whether fixed amounts of compensation paid regularly in intervals of more than one month, and labelled 'bonuses', were required to be included in employees' ordinary wages. The MOEL had advised that such compensation could be excluded from ordinary wage. However, the Supreme Court settled the issue, holding that *all* compensation that is regular, uniform, and fixed/pre-determinable, is part of ordinary wage irrespective of the payment interval or name given.

this notice-or-pay requirement, the most notable of which are for employees still in the first three months of employment, or employees who have caused certain types of significant or wilful harm to their employer as set out by regulation, such as through embezzlement or vandalism.

All employees who have served one year or longer are also entitled to certain severance or retirement benefits upon termination, whether voluntary or involuntary, as discussed further in section 10.2. Payment of benefits or transfer of retirement funds must be effected in full and without setoff (except in very limited circumstances) within fourteen days of termination, or an employer may be criminally liable and face fines and/or imprisonment.[27]

5.3. Fines and Penalties

When dismissing an employee, an employer takes the risk that its justification for the dismissal, or conduct leading up to it, will be found by the Labor Relations Commission or by a competent court to have been deficient. In a proceeding to determine wrongful dismissal, the burden of proof is placed on the employer-defendant, not the employee-plaintiff. The LSA was amended, with effect from 19 November 2021, to make clear that the Labor Relations Commission has authority to hear unjust dismissal claims even if the employee's fixed-term has subsequently expired or the employee has reached the employer's mandatory retirement age – such claims had sometimes been dismissed as moot.[28]

Moreover, the reasons explained in the mandatory notice of dismissal are the reasons that must be defended in any legal proceeding. An employer's ability to proffer additional grounds, without undergoing the entire process again, is sharply limited.

A successful plaintiff in a wrongful termination suit or administrative proceeding is entitled to back wages for the period of unlawful dismissal and reinstatement at the employee's option. In very limited circumstances, such as where a dismissal is in wilful violation of the law, the plaintiff may also be entitled to tort damages for emotional distress. If the Labor Relations Commission orders the reinstatement of an employee but the employer does not reinstate the employee pending appeal, a penalty can be imposed of up to KRW 30 million (increased from KRW 20 million, for terminations that occurred on or after 19 November 2021), two times per year for up to two years, for a total of KRW 120 million. These penalties are refundable if the employer eventually prevails.[29]

27. ERBSA Arts 9, 17(2)–(5), 20(5), 44.
28. LSA Art. 30(4).
29. LSA Art. 33.

Termination of: (i) an employee while that employee is unable to work due to medical treatment of an occupational injury or disease (*see* section 11), and within thirty days thereafter; (ii) a female employee during statutory maternity leave (*see* section 9.8) and within thirty days thereafter; or (iii) an employee on statutory childcare leave (*see* section 10.4), is punishable as a criminal offence, by fine and/or imprisonment.[30]

5.4. Checklist of Do's and Don'ts

- Consider offering fixed-term employment and carefully evaluating an employee's performance before hiring that employee on a permanent basis.
- When drafting rules of employment, ensure disciplinary measures are appropriately detailed and include termination as a potential response to severely deficient or culpable conduct.
- Maintain detailed records of all performance and disciplinary issues.
- Ensure that all wages, benefits, and required severance, are paid in full within fourteen days of termination. Do not apply, without careful review, any setoff for amounts believed to be owed by the employee to the employer.
- In all but the most egregious circumstances, proving that there was 'just cause' to terminate an employee is an inherently difficult and risky enterprise. Therefore, consider offering a reasonable incentive for an employee to voluntarily resign to avoid a potential legal dispute.

6. LAYOFFS, REDUCTIONS IN FORCE, AND/OR REDUNDANCIES AS A RESULT OF JOB ELIMINATIONS OR OTHER RESTRUCTURING

6.1. Overview

As with involuntary termination because of individual fault, involuntary termination as part of a workforce reduction can also only be undertaken for 'just cause'.[31] However, application of the standard differs in this context, and Article 24 of the LSA provides specific statutory requirements that must be met in order for any layoffs to be lawful.

30. LSA Arts 23(2) & 107, EEA Arts 19(3) & 37(2)(3).
31. LSA Art. 23(1).

6.2. Reductions in Force/Layoffs/Job Eliminations

Layoffs for business reasons are permitted only when an employer:

(1) faces an urgent business necessity to reduce its workforce;
(2) makes every effort to avoid dismissing employees;
(3) selects employees to be dismissed based on fair and rational criteria; and
(4) gives fifty days' notice before the intended date of termination, to a union representing a majority of employees, or a representative selected by a majority of employees if no such union exists (either referred to hereafter as an *employee representative*); and consults with the employee representative with respect to the means used to avoid terminating employees and the criteria used to select them for termination.[32]

An urgent business necessity does not necessarily mean that an employer faces imminent bankruptcy in the absence of a workforce reduction; it can also arise because of competitive trends, and future risks to the company in the absence of restructuring. However, it is not an easy standard to meet and requires more than simply the potential for increased profits by reducing labour costs.

'Best efforts' to avoid layoffs is an exacting requirement, which can involve offering affected employees incentives to accept voluntary resignation (also known in Korea as 'voluntary retirement'), attempting to secure third-party employment or internal reassignment for them, instituting a hiring freeze, and reducing working hours, as well as other cost-reduction measures, sales of assets, and more. Such measures targeting employees must, however, be strictly voluntary; use of coercive methods to induce acceptance of voluntary separation may cause it to be seen as involuntary dismissal.

The requirement that laid-off employees be selected using fair and reasonable criteria does not simply mean that explicitly unlawful criteria, such as gender, are not allowed. Rather, it is an affirmative requirement to implement objectively fair criteria in selecting which employees to terminate. Korean courts require that an employer considers both the needs of the employer and its employees in establishing the criteria for termination, and courts have allowed criteria such as age, seniority, number of dependents, and performance to be included in employers' selection process. Although only *consultation* with a union representing a majority of employees (if there is one) or other ad hoc employee representative is required by statute,[33] obtaining labour *consent* to the selection criteria, such

32. LSA Art. 24.
33. LSA Art. 24(3).

as from an employee union, can be a useful way to strengthen the case that they are in fact fair and reasonable.

Failure to strictly adhere to the notice requirement, for example, has been found not to automatically render an employer's terminations unlawful. Instead, the standards are applied in a given case based on the totality of the circumstances.

Where the number of redundancies meets or exceeds certain thresholds, a report must be filed with the MOEL. The reporting threshold is 10% or more of the number of people ordinarily employed by the employer, with a minimum threshold of ten employees and a maximum threshold of one hundred employees.[34] Failure to file the required report does not affect the lawfulness of the employee terminations and does not carry any specific penalties.

An employee dismissed for business reasons is entitled to preferential treatment if an employer intends to hire someone for the same position within three years after the dismissal. Although in practice, this requirement is difficult to enforce.

6.3. Fines and Penalties

As with an individual involuntary termination, an employer who engages in layoffs takes the risk that its justification for the terminations, or conduct leading up to them, will be found to have been deficient by the Labor Relations Commission or by a competent court. The procedural requirements, burden of proof, and potential remedies are the same but applicable to all of the affected employees.

6.4. Checklist of Do's and Don'ts

- Competent legal counsel is highly recommended in the event an employer is considering redundancies. Whether the business rationale for restructuring is sufficiently compelling, or if restructuring may not in fact be a business necessity, must be carefully considered.
- Concerted efforts to avoid involuntary termination are required. These efforts should include things such as internal reassignment, third-party job transfers, and/or voluntary separation packages. However, avoid heavy-handed or coercive methods of inducement that could be seen as constructive termination.
- Comply with union/employee notification and consultation requirements.

34. LSA Enforcement Decree Art. 10(1).

- If layoffs are unavoidable, use fair and objective criteria to determine the employees who must be laid-off.
- Ensure that all wages, benefits, and required severance, are paid in full within fourteen days of termination. Do not apply, without careful review, any setoff for amounts believed to be owed by the employees to the employer.

7. USE OF ALTERNATIVE WORKFORCES: INDEPENDENT CONTRACTORS, CONTRACT EMPLOYEES AND TEMPORARY OR LEASED WORKERS

7.1. OVERVIEW

Under Korean labour law, there are two broad categories of workers: regular and non-regular. They are not legally defined terms but are very frequently used. Regular workers (or regular employees) are full-time employees with indefinite employment terms who work for their legal employer. Employees with an indefinite employment term generally have a right to continued employment until reaching the employer's mandatory retirement age, unless terminated for 'just cause'. Since terminating an employment relationship with an indefinite-term employee before the employee reaches retirement age is a challenging task in Korea – which generally does not allow 'at-will' employment – they are often referred to as 'permanent' (as opposed to fixed-term) employees.

There are four principal types of non-regular workers: (i) part-time employees, (ii) fixed-term employees, (iii) dispatched workers from manpower supply agencies, and (iv) subcontracted workers and independent contractors. The first two refer to individuals who work under the direct supervision and control of the relevant business and are treated as its legal employees. The third refers to individuals who work under the direct supervision and control of the relevant business but *are not* treated as its legal employees, due to compliance with the worker-dispatch law, the DWA. The last refers to workers who *do not* work under the direct supervision and control of the relevant business, and thus are not treated as its legal employees.

The FTPTA and the DWA govern the relationship between an employer and its non-regular employees, and between a using business and its dispatched workers, respectively.

7.2. Fixed-Term and Part-Time Employees

Under the FTPTA,[35] a fixed-term employee is one whose term of employment is limited to a specific period of time not in excess of two years. After two years of continuous service with an employer, subject to some exceptions,[36] a fixed-term employee will become a regular, permanent employee by operation of law,[37] entitled to continued employment until reaching retirement age absent 'just cause' for termination.

A part-time employee is one whose contractual working hours are fewer than a comparable full-time employee at the same workplace.[38] Part-time employment can be for a fixed term or for an indefinite term. However, a part-time employee whose average weekly working hours (averaged over four weeks) are under fifteen is excluded from application of the rule under the FTPTA by which a fixed-term employee becomes permanent after serving for two years.

Overtime work for part-time employees is limited to twelve hours per week. Further, a part-time employee has a right to refuse overtime work if the employer has not obtained prior consent.[39]

The employment contract or statement of written employment terms for part-time and fixed-term employees are subject to special requirements (*see* section 2).

Both fixed-term employees and part-time employees are eligible to receive severance or retirement benefits from a company in a manner equivalent to regular employees if they are employed continuously in excess of one year. However, part-time employees whose average weekly working hours (averaged over four weeks) are under fifteen are excluded from this entitlement.

7.3. Independent Contractors

It is permissible under Korean law to engage the services of an individual as an independent contractor rather than a statutory employee. However, if the substance of the relationship is, under the totality of the circumstances, that of an employee and employer, under Korean law, the individual will be

35. The FTPTA generally applies to all employers with at least five employees, except for domestic employees.
36. Some notable exceptions to this rule include certain jobs requiring professional knowledge and skills, such as attorneys and medical doctors; certain managerial jobs where the compensation exceeds a certain regulatory threshold; and jobs defined by a specific project requiring more than two years to complete.
37. FTPTA Art. 4(2).
38. FTPTA Art. 2.
39. FTPTA Art. 6(2).

deemed an employee irrespective of the language used in the relevant contract. A variety of factors including the exercise of direct supervision and control over an individual purporting to be an independent contractor, along with other factors such as tax treatment (e.g., whether value-added tax (VAT) is paid), may be suggestive of the individual being a de facto employee.

One area in which this issue frequently arises is in the context of registered directors (i.e., members of the board). Board members are not, solely by virtue of fulfilling their responsibility to manage the business, considered to be 'employees' within the scope of the LSA. This is because directors are seen as exercising their own discretion in directing the management of the business. However, if a director appears in substance to be performing work under the direction of the business, there is the potential that the director can be found to be an employee, entitling the individual to all the protections of the LSA, including the right to continued employment (though not to continued membership on the board).

There is an ongoing debate over whether so-called platform workers (e.g., couriers, drivers, and others who utilize a work-assignment platform to connect with customers/clients) are 'employees' under the LSA and TULRAA. Platform workers overall have distinct characteristics compared to ordinary employees (relatively low exclusivity, intermittent periods of work, autonomy and independence over where/when to provide work), which makes it difficult and complex to directly apply the LSA and TULRAA. There are continuous legislative efforts to address such limitations.

7.4. Leased or Dispatched Workers

Under the DWA, there are certain enumerated job categories – generally of an ancillary business nature (e.g., drivers, receptionists, security guards) – for which an employer can hire dispatched workers through a 'worker-dispatch agency' (also referred to as a 'manpower supply agency'), and use their labour under its own supervision and control.[40] Dispatched workers may not be used for longer than two years, or they acquire the right to demand regular, permanent employment by the using business.

If a company uses dispatched workers for an impermissible role under the DWA, the violation can result in criminal sanctions of up to three years of imprisonment or a KRW 30 million fine, imposed upon both the service recipient business (and its registered representative) and the manpower

40. For example, the use of dispatched workers in direct production-line jobs in the manufacturing industry is not permitted under the DWA. Dispatched workers can also be used as temporary replacements for employees absent for certain enumerated reasons (e.g., childbirth), even in a role that is not specifically permitted, so long as they do not work in a *prohibited* role.

supply agency. Moreover, the service recipient business will be obligated to directly hire the dispatched worker as its own employee immediately, even if the dispatch term does not exceed two years if the dispatch is deemed to be illegal. When a service recipient business is required to directly hire dispatched workers, those workers are entitled to receive the same terms and conditions as existing employees performing similar duties or, if there are no existing employees performing similar duties, they are entitled to maintain their existing terms and conditions.[41]

On 27 January 2022, the Supreme Court held that absent special circumstances, illegally dispatched workers who are required to be directly hired by the using company are entitled to indefinite-term employment rather than fixed-term employment.[42] The burden of proof that there are special circumstances – such as that the particular outsourced workers would normally be on a fixed-term contract – would be borne by the employer.

7.5. Contract, Subcontracted or Outsourced Workers

It is not an uncommon practice in Korea for a company to bring in employees of a third-party service provider, more commonly referred to as a 'contractor' or 'subcontractor', to work at the company's workplace or site. However, in order for them to be recognized as 'subcontracted workers', they must be subject to the supervision and control of the third-party employer, rather than that of the company receiving their services. In this sense, the legal considerations respecting subcontracted labour are similar to those relating to independent contractors, but with the intermediation of another employer. Thus, a business must be careful not to interfere with the third-party service provider's supervision and control of its employees, to avoid running a high risk of the arrangement being deemed a de facto worker dispatch, subject to the requirements of the DWA and the concomitant danger of the workers being deemed direct employees. There is no time limit on the use of subcontracted or outsourced labour, so long as the workers are not subject to the using company's supervision and control to such a degree that they appear to be its direct employees.

7.6. Discrimination Against Non-regular Workers

Employers cannot treat non-regular workers (including fixed-term employees, part-time employees, and dispatched workers) disadvantageously compared to regular workers with respect to wages and

41. DWA Art. 6-2(3).
42. S. Ct. Case No. 2018Da207847 (27 Jan. 2022).

other working conditions, without reasonable grounds. The FTPTA's legal definition and scope of prohibited discriminatory treatment include all matters related to wages, bonuses, and other working conditions and welfare benefits.[43] The act does not oblige employers to provide precisely equal treatment to regular and non-regular workers with respect to all terms of employment, but it bans discriminatory treatment without reasonable justification. Thus, different treatment of non-regular workers is permitted when there are reasonable grounds such as differences in productivity and skills.

Formerly, to obtain review of unreasonably discriminatory treatment, non-regular workers were required to actively seek redress, generally by filing a complaint with the Labor Relations Commission. However, due to amendments to the FTPTA and DWA, the MOEL can independently initiate investigations of employers to ensure that there are no discriminatory practices, even in the absence of any complaint. These amendments also make treble damages available (as a punitive measure) to employees damaged by such discrimination if it is intentional or repeated.[44]

If an employer does not comply with the MOEL's corrective instructions, if any are issued, the MOEL will formally file a complaint to the National Labor Relations Commission, which will then conduct its own investigation to determine the merits of the case and issue a corrective order. A penalty of up to KRW 100 million may be imposed for non-compliance with the Commission's corrective order. Due to recent amendments to the law, even if the corrective order from the Labor Relations Commission applies only to one employee, the MOEL may expand the order to other similarly situated employees.

7.7. Checklist of Do's and Don'ts

- Track the service periods of all fixed-term employees (and dispatched workers, if applicable), and only allow them to work for more than two years if intending to offer them permanent employment (or if an exemption applies).
- Only hire dispatched workers through reputable dispatch agencies, and take care to comply with all applicable laws so as to avoid inadvertently hiring a permanent employee by operation of law.

43. *See* FTPTA Art. 2(3).
44. In 2016, for the first time a court actually approved holding a worker-dispatch agency and using employer jointly liable for punitive damages – equivalent to double the amount of actual damages – based on intentional or repeated discrimination against dispatched workers. *See* Case No. 2015Guhap70416 (Seoul Admin. Ct. 18 Nov. 2016), *aff'd*, Case No. 2016Nu79078 (Seoul High Ct. 17 May 2017).

- Take precautions to minimize the risk that a subcontractor's workers may be deemed illegally dispatched workers or direct employees. This requires maintaining the distinct and separate identities of both the using business and service provider, as well as each business's employees. The primary means of doing so is to avoid exerting too much direct supervision or control over the operation of the subcontractor's employees.
- Specific useful precautions to keep in mind include avoiding situations where a subcontractor's employees work together at the same location, do identical work, wear the same uniforms, or otherwise project an image that is not meaningfully distinct from the company's own employees. The using business and the subcontractor should also have separate formal corporate identities, without excessive control or intermingling. Although the using business may specify the nature of the services it needs, it should not control the exact methods by which the purchased services are delivered; it is important that the subcontractor is not merely a conduit through which the using business controls the individual employees.

8. OBLIGATION TO BARGAIN COLLECTIVELY WITH TRADE UNIONS: EMPLOYEES' RIGHT TO STRIKE AND A COMPANY'S RIGHT TO CONTINUE BUSINESS OPERATIONS

8.1. Overview of Unions' Right to Organize

The right of private-sector workers to independent association, collective bargaining, and collective action are all enshrined in Article 33 of the Korean Constitution.[45] These rights are given form by the TULRAA, which sets out the specific rules by which labour unions may be formed and governed, and by which they may enter into CBAs. The legal hurdles to organizing a union are not particularly high. Since 1 July 2011, a single employer or workplace may have multiple employee unions, and those unions may be formed without any election being held beforehand; the minimum required number of union members is only two. Despite the ease with which unions may be formed, Korea's union density is relatively low compared to other Organisation for Economic Co-operation and Development (OECD) countries; it was found to be just over 14.2% as of 2021,[46] and union

45. Article 33 of the Constitution states that collective bargaining by public officials is allowed to the extent provided by act, and union formation and bargaining by such officials is governed by the Public Officials' Trade Union Act. Article 33 also provides that the right of workers to collectively bargain may be curtailed by statute if they are employed in important defence-related industries.

46. According to the MOEL, it is 14.2% as of the end of 2021. https://www.moel.go.kr/news/enews/report/enewsView.do?news_seq=14436.

membership is more concentrated in the public sector than the private sector with a 70.0% public-sector rate versus an 11.2% private-sector rate.

It is permissible to form enterprise-level or industry-level unions, as well as confederations of individual unions.

Employers that regularly employ thirty or more people are also required to establish a labour-management council, but this council is not empowered to engage in collective bargaining like a union. However, consultation or resolution through the labour-management council is mandated for a variety of employment-related matters. Employers of this size must also constitute a grievance-handling committee with up to three grievance officers from each of the employer and employees; at any workplace with a labour-management council, they must be chosen from among the council's members.[47]

8.2. Right of Employees to Form and Join Unions

Employees may freely form and join a union, and a union may not discriminate against any eligible employee who wishes to join, on the basis of race, religion, gender, age, physical condition, type of employment, political party, or social status.[48]

Employers may not make it a condition of employment that a worker join or abstain from joining, a union; *unless* the employer and a union representing more than two-thirds of the employees in the same business agree to a 'union shop' provision in a CBA, in which case new employees may be required to join the union but cannot be disadvantaged if they are expelled from the union, or withdraw to organize or join a different union.[49]

To establish a union, an employee must prepare a report with certain statutorily required information and submit it, along with the union's by-laws, to a local government or the MOEL depending on the type and scope of the union. A certificate recognizing the union must be issued within three days of the submission, or a request to supplement the report may be issued instead, in which case certification must be granted within three days of submission of a supplemented report. Certification may generally be denied only if requested supplemental information is not provided, or if the proposed union organization is not of a type that may properly be recognized as a union. Such improper union organizations include 'company unions', to which the employer provides a majority of the required financial support, or in which the employer's management is allowed membership; unions which

47. Promotion of Workers' Participation and Cooperation Act.
48. TULRAA Arts 5 & 9.
49. TULRAA Art. 81(2).

allow membership to individuals who are not workers; and organizations which are primarily political in nature.[50]

There has long been a strict requirement allowing only 'employees' to be members of an enterprise union, with a limited exception allowing continued membership by a dismissed employee while the employee disputes the dismissal, if the employee accuses the employer of unfair labour practices. However, under recent amendments to the TULRAA, effective since 6 July 2021, it became possible for non-employees to join enterprise unions and participate in their activities, subject to certain significant limitations: they cannot serve as union officers, they do not count when voting for industrial action, and they can only engage in union activity at the employer's workplace if it does not 'adversely affect' the operation of the business. There are ongoing disputes regarding whether and when independent contractors can unionize and be proper counterparties in collective bargaining and whether and when companies can be proper collective-bargaining counterparties in relation to workers employed by subcontractors. In a notable development, on 12 January 2023, the Seoul Administrative Court held that a subcontractor's employees were entitled to collectively bargain with the service-recipient business because it had the authority to control and determine the terms and conditions of those employees in a practical and concrete manner.[51] This is a controversial area that is still developing, and will likely be addressed by the Supreme Court in the future.

With regard to public enterprises and quasi-government institutions under the recently amended Act on the Management of Public Institutions (AMPI), effective 4 August 2022, such institutions will be required to appoint a 'worker director'[52] to be included among their non-standing directors.[53] A 'worker director' must be an employee who has been employed by such institution for at least three years and is recommended by the employee representative (if there is a majority union, the head of such union shall be the employee representative) or approved by a majority of the employees.[54]

8.3. Multiple Unions and the Bargaining Representative

Forming a union is a relatively easy process, multiple unions may be formed in a single enterprise or workplace, and eligible employees are generally free to join or not join any particular union, as discussed above. However, two

50. TULRAA Arts 2(4) & 12.
51. *See* Case No. 2021Guhap71748 (Seoul Admin. Ct. 12 Jan. 2023).
52. Literally translated, 'labour director'.
53. AMPI Arts 25, 26 (effective 4 Aug. 2022).
54. AMPRI Art. 25.

legal principles make collective decision-making by employees of significant importance.

First, a CBA will only apply generally, even to workers who are not members of the union that negotiated it, in two circumstances: (i) if it applies to at least half of the employees, or a particular class of employees, in a single enterprise or workplace, it will apply to all other such employees; and (ii) if it applies to more than two-thirds of the workers performing the same kind of job and employed in the same geographical area, the Labor Relations Commission may declare that it applies to all other such workers.[55]

Second, generally, a union may only negotiate on behalf of its own members, and an employer is only required to enter collective bargaining in a single bargaining channel (although an employer may *consent* to collective bargaining with multiple unions). Therefore, if there are multiple unions representing the employees of a given employer, the TULRAA provides that they must undergo a statutory process to designate one union or a group of individuals from multiple unions, as the sole 'bargaining representative', in order to negotiate a CBA with the employer.

Because of these two principles, for a CBA to have general force throughout an employer's workforce or over an entire class of employees, it must be negotiated by either: (i) a union representing at least half of the total employees or the class of employees sought to be covered; or (ii) a bargaining representative selected from among unions that represent at least half of such employees.

Until recently, the maximum duration of a CBA was two years, and collective bargaining to enter into a CBA would usually occur every two years, with collective bargaining on a more limited wage agreement occurring annually. However, the maximum effective period of a CBA has been increased from two to three years.[56]

8.4. Unfair Labour Practices

Unfair labour practices are prohibited by the TULRAA and are subject to criminal penalties of up to two years of imprisonment or KRW 20 million. The TULRAA defines 'unfair labour practices' to include:

(i) dismissing or discriminating against workers for joining, intending to join or establish, or performing any lawful act for the operation of a union;

55. TULRAA Arts 35–36.
56. TULRAA Art. 32.

(ii) conditioning employment on joining or abstaining from joining a union (except where agreed in a CBA with a union representing more than two-thirds of employees);
(iii) refusing or delaying required collective bargaining without justifiable reasons;
(iv) dominating or interfering with the formation or operation of a union, or financially supporting a union, except for certain permissible means of support, such as time off for union activities during working hours, and union offices on company premises; and
(v) dismissing or discriminating against workers for engaging in lawful industrial actions and reporting or testifying about violations of the TULRAA.

Dominating or interfering with union activities is interpreted in a manner highly protective of free and independent union activity organized by the employees themselves. Accordingly, overt efforts to persuade or dissuade employees from forming a union, operating a union in a certain way, or adopting a certain course of collective action, are quite strongly discouraged and carry significant risk. This includes efforts to influence the election of union leadership, decisions to engage in industrial action or election of a bargaining representative.

Paying employees for their time dedicated to union activities is allowed only within limits set by law and regulation, which are based on workforce size. It is an unfair labour practice to pay for more such union-related time off than the total amount provided under this system.

8.5. Subjects of Collective Bargaining and Industrial Action

Korean law, like that of other jurisdictions, mandates that collective bargaining be conducted in good faith with respect to certain subjects (mandatory subjects), permits bargaining to be conducted with respect to certain other subjects (permissive subjects), and prohibits any collective agreement between an employer and union with respect to other subjects (prohibited subjects).

Mandatory subjects of collective bargaining are primarily general working conditions, including wages, working hours, holidays, vacations, accident compensation, and worker safety. Dismissals of employees are not, themselves, mandatory subjects of collective bargaining; however, the general procedures and justifications for dismissals are. Refusal to negotiate in good faith with respect to mandatory subjects is an unfair labour practice, and a deadlock can be a justification for lawful industrial action. Permissive subjects generally are related to labour-management relations such as union activities, deduction of union dues, and the treatment of full-time union officials; an employer's refusal to negotiate permissive subjects is not an unfair labour practice, and cannot justify lawful industrial action. Prohibited subjects are primarily matters that are otherwise prohibited by law, and thus not subject to any contrary agreement, such as lowering working standards below the minimum mandated by Korean labour law; prohibited subjects may not be negotiated and cannot be agreed upon in a CBA.

The Supreme Court has held[57] that an employer is not obligated to negotiate with a union over restructuring or layoffs, which are inherently subject to the decision of the management; however, if the employer negotiates and enters into a CBA limiting its power to carry out layoffs in the future, it should be respected. As a result, the Court concluded that an employer's layoffs in violation of such an agreement are illegal, except where there are special circumstances justifying the employer's failure to abide by the agreement (such as an unexpected serious financial crisis).

If the negotiating parties are unable to reach an agreement on a mandatory subject of collective bargaining, the parties must undergo a statutorily required mediation process or such other conciliation process as they mutually agree or provide for in their CBA. The statutory mediation process begins when one party submits a request to the Labor Relations Commission and is to be complete within ten or fifteen days, for general businesses and public services, respectively, and subject to extension for up to the same amount of time by agreement. The parties may also agree to binding arbitration by the Labor Relations Commission. Industrial action is only permitted if no resolution is reached during the time period for mediation, or after fifteen days from the date of any referral to arbitration by the Labor Relations Commission. Hiring replacement workers during lawful industrial action is not permitted, with limited exceptions.

The law also provides for mutually agreed private mediation/arbitration in lieu of utilizing the Labor Relations Commission for that purpose.

8.6. Checklist of Do's and Don'ts

- Avoid any statements or acts that appear aimed at influencing the decision-making of employees with respect to union activities, such as forming a union, or electing its representatives.
- Future scrutiny of an employer's collection of information about its employees' labour-union-related activities will be heightened. There are court precedents in which courts have declared that if an employer has

57. S. Ct. Case No. 2011Du20406 (27 Mar. 2014).

collected information on labour union activities by shadowing its members with the intent to prevent the members from actively participating in union activities, this act itself constitutes 'interfering with the formation or operation of a union', which is an unfair labour practice, even if the shadowed members were unaware of the surveillance.

- When considering an adverse employment action such as termination, suspension, or demotion, if the employee is involved in union-related activities consider whether the act could be seen as a punishment for such activities. Unlike regular unjust termination, unfair labour practices carry criminal penalties including imprisonment.
- A CBA ranks highly in the hierarchy of sources of binding employment rules. This hierarchy is generally: laws > CBAs > work rules > individual employment agreements. Thus, a provision in a business's work rules or in an individual employment contract may be overridden by a contrary provision in any applicable CBA. Therefore, CBAs should not only be carefully negotiated in the first place but also receive close attention in developing and establishing any other work policies and practices.

9. WORKING CONDITIONS: HOURS OF WORK AND PAYMENT OF WAGES: BY STATUTE OR COLLECTIVE AGREEMENTS

9.1. Overview of Wage and Hours Laws

The two most important sources of Korean wage and hours laws are the LSA and the MWA. The MWA applies to all employers except those who employ only relatives living together with the employer, and to every type of employee except household/domestic employees.[58] Certain LSA provisions are applicable even to employers with fewer than five employees, as noted in section 1.2, and these provisions include some that relate to working hours, wages, recess time, and weekly days off. However, the LSA's provisions on working hours, recess time, and weekly days off are almost entirely inapplicable to certain categories of employment, particularly agricultural or forestry work, livestock breeding, fishery, surveillance or intermittent work (with approval from the MOEL), and high-level managerial and supervisory work or work involving handling highly sensitive confidential information.[59] Note that the exemption for employees handling managerial and supervisory work or highly sensitive confidential information is interpreted very narrowly.

58. MWA Art. 3. Seamen subject to the Seaman Act, and their ship-owner employers, are also exempt.
59. LSA Art. 63, LSA Enforcement Decree Art. 34.

9.2. Minimum Wage

Korea's minimum wage is determined by the MOEL each year by 5 August, through a process involving deliberations by the tripartite (labour, business, public) Minimum Wage Council, as well as public notice and comment.[60]

The MOEL may exclude certain types of wages from the wages that are counted in determining whether an employee's compensation meets the minimum wage requirement; these excludable wages include those paid irregularly or in intervals of more than one month, as well as wages paid for overtime work or work during days off.

The MWA was amended such that, effective as of 1 January 2019, bonuses and welfare benefits paid on a regular monthly basis are considered as wages for determining minimum-wage compliance, to the extent that they exceed a certain percentage (initially 25% and 7%, respectively) of the monthly minimum wage for the year. The percentages are being lowered progressively each year up to 2024 when all regular monthly paid bonuses and welfare benefits will be included in the wage calculation:

Percentages That Are Not Counted as Minimum Wage

Year	2019	2020	2021	2022	2023	2024
Bonus (paid on a monthly basis)	25%	20%	15%	10%	5%	0%
Cash Welfare Benefits	7%	5%	3%	2%	1%	0%

If an employer intends to amend its rules of employment to adjust the intervals of payments to convert them to monthly payments, so as to ensure that the payments are incorporated into the wage calculation for determining minimum-wage compliance, a workforce consultation – with a majority trade union, if any, or with the majority of the employees if there is no majority union – will still be required. Still, majority consent will not be necessary so long as the total amount of the payment is unchanged.[61]

The minimum wage for 2023 is KRW 9,620 per hour (a 5.02% increase from 2022). The statutory working hours used for calculating minimum-wage compliance – i.e., into which wages are divided to obtain an

60. MWA Arts 8, 9, 12 & 14.
61. MWA Art. 6-2.

hourly wage – include a day's worth of working hours per statutory paid day off but *exclude* other *non-mandatory* paid days off.[62]

The minimum wage for employees who are in the first three months of a probationary period (except those employed on a fixed-term contract with a term of less than one year) is 90% of the normal minimum wage.[63] However, it is impermissible to reduce wages for 'simple labour' workers – workers performing unskilled labour within a scope defined by the MOEL – based on their being in a probationary period.[64] A probationary period is a common mechanism used in Korea to evaluate employee performance over a limited time, such as three or six months, and during a probationary period, courts apply the 'just cause' requirement for termination somewhat more leniently. However, employees still enjoy significant job protection.

All employers covered by the MWA must pay at least the minimum wage to covered employees and must not lower previous wage levels on account of a change in the minimum wage, or they can face criminal penalties of up to three years of imprisonment or a fine of up to KRW 20 million.[65]

9.3. Overtime

Employers who ordinarily employ five or more employees are subject to the LSA's maximum-hours and overtime requirements. There are multiple systems for determining the maximum regular (non-overtime) daily or weekly working hours that may apply to an employee.

For full-time employees, generally, any hours worked beyond the maximum daily or weekly regular working hours under the applicable system constitute overtime. However, for part-time employees, 'overtime' means any hours in excess of their normal contractual working hours.[66]

As discussed below, certain categories of employees are particularly restricted in the number of overtime hours they are permitted to work. For example, pregnant employees are not allowed to work any overtime hours at all, even at their request.

Employees who are not among those protected classes, however, may work twelve overtime hours per week (or an average of twelve overtime hours per week under the 'selective-hours' system discussed below).[67]

62. The LSA requires one paid day off per week, so in effect this will mean that any additional paid days off per week (e.g., the other day of the weekend) will not count towards the denominator when calculating an employee's hourly wage for minimum-wage compliance purposes.
63. MWA Art. 5(2), MWA Enforcement Decree Art. 3(1).
64. MWA Art. 5(2).
65. MWA Arts 6(1)–(2) & 28(1).
66. *But see* Note on fifty-two-hour week LSA amendments, below.
67. LSA Art. 53(1) & (2), FTPTA Art. 6(1)–(2). Additional overtime is possible in limited circumstances with approval of the MOEL. LSA Art. 53(4).

Employees cannot be unilaterally required to work overtime but may work overtime if they have agreed to do so. More than twelve hours of overtime is generally only permissible with MOEL approval or, under exigent circumstances, post-facto MOEL approval.

Until recently, however, MOEL regulations limited these 'exigent circumstances' only to situations where extra overtime was necessary to respond to a natural disaster, emergency, or similarly severe incident. However, the MOEL issued new regulations effective 31 January 2020, which expanded the scope of 'special circumstances' justifying extra overtime. Responding to a natural disaster or other emergency has been expanded to include preventing one, and four entirely new grounds have been added.[68]

Employers in enumerated industries are, however, permitted to agree with the employee representative to extend overtime hours beyond twelve, as well as to alter the mandatory statutory recess periods.[69]

(i) Overtime work; (ii) work between 10:00 p.m. and 6:00 a.m. (referred to as 'night work'); and (iii) work during days off (also referred to as 'holiday work') each requires additional pay of 50% of an employee's ordinary wage, generally cumulatively.[70] Employers may compensate workers for overtime work, night work, and work during days off, by providing additional leave instead of monetary compensation, but only under a written agreement with the employee representative.[71]

The permissible systems for determining an employee's maximum regular weekly working hours (i.e., not including overtime or, under the MOEL interpretation discussed above, weekend work) are as follows.

---

68. According to the LSA Enforcement Decree Art. 9(1), any of the following 'special circumstances' justify an application for extra overtime:

    (1) Where necessary to take urgent action to prevent or respond to a natural disaster, emergency, or other similarly severe incident, or limit the damage therefrom.
    (2) Where necessary to take urgent actions to protect life or secure safety.
    (3) Where necessary to take urgent actions to control damage from emergency situations, including the malfunctioning of facilities and equipment.
    (4) Where there is an unusual heavy increase in workload that could lead to material hindrance or damage to the business if not resolved quickly.
    (5) Where research and development is being conducted, such as research and development of materials and components and of facilities for manufacturing materials and components, that the Minister of Employment and Labor recognizes as being necessary to strengthen national competitiveness, etc.

69. LSA Art. 59.
70. LSA Art. 56.
71. LSA Art. 57.

9.3.1. Standard Hours System

In the absence of any agreement or company rules to the contrary, the maximum regular (non-overtime) working hours that may be agreed to by contract are eight hours per day, and forty hours per week, each exclusive of statutory rest periods discussed below in section 9.4.[72]

9.3.2. Flexible Hours System

Three types of 'flexible hours' systems are available for non-pregnant employees who are at least 18 years old.[73,74]

Type 1 (two-week average): Employees may work up to forty-eight regular working hours in any one week, and subtract an equivalent amount of regular working hours from the next week so that the average over two weeks is not more than forty regular working hours. This system must be provided for in company rules or regulations.

Type 2 (up to three-month average): Employees may work up to fifty-two regular working hours per week, and twelve per day, so long as regular working hours per week are forty or less when averaged over a calculation period of up to three months. This arrangement must be agreed upon with the employee representative, in writing, specifying specific terms enumerated by statute.

Type 3 (more than three-month, up to six-month average): On 5 January 2021, the LSA was amended, with effect from 6 April 2021 for an employer with fifty or more employees and from 1 July 2021 for an employer with five or more but less than fifty employees, to expand the maximum flexible hours calculation period to six months. This arrangement must be agreed upon with an employee representative in writing. And when agreeing upon a calculation period of more than three months and up to six months, daily working hours should be decided on weekly intervals, and employees should be notified of the schedule at least two weeks beforehand. Moreover, the employer should give at least eleven consecutive hours of rest between work days. In addition, to prevent any potential pay cut due to the expansion of the calculation period, an employer should prepare an agenda to preserve wages and report it to the MOEL.

72. LSA Art. 50.
73. LSA Art. 51.
74. LSA Art. 51-2.

9.3.3. Selective-Hours System

A 'selective-hours' system is available for employees who are at least 18 years old, even if pregnant.[75]

Employees with some measure of discretion over their starting and finishing times may work an unlimited number of regular working hours per week and per day, so long as the average regular working hours per week are forty or less when averaged over a period of up to one month. This arrangement must be agreed upon with the employee representative, in writing, specifying specific terms enumerated by statute.

On 5 January 2021, the LSA was amended, with effect from 6 April 2021 for an employer with fifty or more employees and from 1 July 2021 for an employer with five or more but less than fifty employees, to increase the maximum calculation period for the selective-hours system up to three months for employees engaged in the development of new products or technology. This arrangement must be agreed upon with an employee representative in writing. If a calculation period exceeding one month is used, the employer must provide eleven consecutive hours of rest between work days and pay an additional allowance (50% of ordinary wage) for hours exceeding forty hours per week on an average basis in a given month during the (up to) three-month period.

9.3.4. Special Rules for Calculating Overtime

There are a number of special rules for calculating the number of hours worked, for purposes of determining an employee's entitlement to overtime pay. Employees who work wholly or partially outside the workplace (e.g., due to business travel or otherwise) may be subject to special rules for calculating or deeming the number of hours worked for purposes of determining an employee's entitlement to overtime pay. This can be an amount pre-agreed in writing with the employee representative.[76] And those who perform certain types of work involving significant discretion over the manner and timing of their work may, if agreed in writing with the employee representative, be deemed to work for such hours as provided in the agreement.[77]

Note on fifty-two-hour week LSA amendments

A law was passed by the National Assembly on 29 February 2018, and promulgated on 20 March 2018, amending the LSA in order to prospectively

75. LSA Art. 52.
76. LSA Art. 58(1)–(2).
77. LSA Art. 58(3), LSA Enforcement Decree Art. 31.

settle a controversy over the proper treatment of work on days off under Korea's overtime rules.

The MOEL had long held that hours worked on regular days off – which generally include one or both days of the weekend – do not count towards the weekly regular-hours limit of forty. This interpretation essentially allows up to eight hours of work per day on the weekend, which does not count as overtime.

The effect of this interpretation was twofold. First, it allowed a maximum workweek of sixty-eight hours (consisting of forty regular hours, twelve overtime hours, and sixteen weekend hours), instead of fifty-two hours (consisting of forty regular hours and twelve overtime hours). Second, it reduced the premium pay required for hours worked on days off, after having worked a forty-hour regular week. This reduction in premium pay occurs because the premium required for overtime, night time, and day-off work (50% each) is generally cumulative, but eight hours of work per regular day off (e.g., Saturday and Sunday) is, by definition, not overtime under this approach.

This interpretation had been controversial, and several lower-court decisions had held it to be contrary to the law. The Supreme Court ultimately decided that the MOEL's interpretation was the correct interpretation of the pre-amendment law.[78]

Under the 2018 amendments, however, the maximum weekly working hours are fifty-two, consisting of forty regular hours and twelve overtime hours. A sixty-eight-hour workweek, consisting of forty regular hours, twelve overtime hours, and up to sixteen day-off (weekend) hours, is no longer possible for most employers.

Premium pay continues to work mostly as it did under the original MOEL interpretation that was challenged in the courts. For work on regular days off – which generally includes one or both days of the weekend – the premium will be only 50% for the first eight hours of each day, even if the employee has already reached the forty-hour weekly regular-hours limit. An additional cumulative 50% overtime premium will only be earned for work beyond eight hours on a regular day off.

The new fifty-two-hour workweek was phased in based on employer size. It became effective on 1 July 2018 for employers with 300+ employees, as well as most government-invested or government-controlled employers; then on 1 January 2020 for employers with 50–299 employees (but with a one-year enforcement grace period giving such employers until 1 January 2021 to comply); and finally it became effective on 1 July 2021 for employers with 5–49 employees. Employers with fewer than five employees are exempt.

78. S. Ct. Case No. 2011Da112391 (en banc decision) (21 Jun. 2011).

9.4. Meal and Rest Periods

All employees must be allowed a rest period of at least thirty minutes for every four working hours, and at least one hour for every eight working hours, to be used freely by the employees.[79]

9.5. Deductions from Wages

Wages must be paid in full to employees, in cash. However, in very limited circumstances such as where provided for by statute or CBA, wages may be subject to partial deductions or paid other than in cash. Wages other than certain extraordinary wages and allowances must be paid at least monthly on a fixed day.[80]

The primary statutorily mandated deductions are for national and local taxes, as well as for national health insurance premiums; social security (national pension) premiums; unemployment insurance premiums; industrial accident insurance premiums; and long-term care insurance premiums. Some of these require an employer contribution as well, while there are other government programmes that are exclusively employer funded.

Korea used to have no specific requirement to issue payslips. However, from 19 November 2021, an employer must issue a payslip to each employee in written form (including electronic form) on each monthly pay day. It must contain (1) information identifying the paid employee, such as name, date of birth, employee number, etc.; (2) the payment date; (3) the total amount of payment; (4) the amount of each payment item, such as basic salary, allowances, bonuses, incentives; (5) the method of calculation of payment items when the amount varies depending on the number of days, hours, etc. (actual working hours should be specified respecting the amount paid for overtime/day-off/night-time work); and (6) if there are any amounts deducted, the details of those deductions, such as each deduction item, and each amount and the total amount of deductions.[81]

9.6. Garnishment

A judgment creditor may obtain a court order for garnishment of an employee's wages under the Civil Execution Act (CEA). The amount subject

79. LSA Art. 54(1).
80. LSA Art. 43. Extraordinary wages and allowances that do not need to be paid monthly, comprise: (i) allowances for good attendance for a period exceeding one month; (ii) seniority allowances paid for consecutive service for a fixed period exceeding one month; (iii) incentives or bonuses calculated based on a period exceeding one month; and (iv) other various allowances not paid on a regular basis. LSA Enforcement Decree Art. 23.
81. LSA Art. 48(2), LSA Enforcement Decree Art. 27-2.

to garnishment is generally half of the employee's wages, but if the employee's wages are above or below certain thresholds set by regulation, the amount subject to garnishment may be greater or lower than that.[82]

9.7. Exemptions to Wage and Hour Laws

Household/domestic employees, and businesses which consist only of relatives living together, are exempt from the LSA, the FTPTA, the MWA, and the EEA.[83] Such businesses and employees are thus free from virtually all regulation of wages and hours, although applicable anti-discrimination laws may indirectly impose restrictions in those areas.

Moreover, all of the LSA's provisions on working hours, recess time, and days off, are entirely inapplicable to certain categories of employment, particularly various kinds of agricultural and forestry work, aqua cultural work and harvesting marine organisms; livestock breeding and sericulture; surveillance or intermittent work (with approval of the MOEL); and high-level managerial and supervisory work or work involving handling highly sensitive confidential information.[84]

Even outside those specific categories of work, employers who ordinarily employ fewer than five people are exempt from many provisions of the relevant labour statutes. Such employers are still required to provide the statutorily required rest periods and weekly days off described in sections 9.4 and 10.3 and to pay extra wages for work beyond regular contractual hours (though, without applying any premium rate), if otherwise applicable. However, these employers are exempt from all of the LSA's other generally applicable restrictions on overtime and nighttime work and work during days off.[85]

Employers with fewer than five employees are still subject to most of the LSA's special protections for women and minors (*see* section 9.8 below). However, they are not required to: (i) provide nursing breaks or time off for pre-natal check-ups; or (ii) obtain consent from a woman who is not pregnant, nursing, or a minor, before that woman may perform any work between 10:00 p.m. and 6:00 a.m. or during days off.[86]

---

82. CEA Art. 246(1)(4).
83. LSA Art. 11(1), FTPTA Art. 3(1), MWA Art. 3(1), EEA Art. 3(1), EEA Enforcement Decree Art. 2(1).
84. LSA Art. 63, LSA Enforcement Decree Art. 34.
85. LSA Art. 11(2), LSA Enforcement Decree Art. 7 & Table 1.
86. LSA Arts 11(2), 70(1)–(2) & 74-2, 75, LSA Enforcement Decree Art. 7 & Table 1.

9.8. Child Labour and Protections for Female Employees

Individuals under 18 years of age (*minors*) are subject to special labour law protections under Chapter V of the LSA. Individuals under the age of 15, as well as individuals under the age of 18 but still enrolled in compulsory middle school (7th to 9th grade), may only be employed if they apply for and receive an employment permit from the MOEL.[87] An employer must keep, in the workplace, the employment certificate or other certification of each minor employee's parent or guardian's consent to their employment.[88] Moreover, a parent, guardian, or the MOEL, are all empowered to terminate any labour contract that is disadvantageous to a minor.[89] Minors are subject to special limits on regular and overtime working hours.[90]

Female employees are also subject to additional protections under Chapter V of the LSA. Women may not be required to work between 10:00 p.m. and 6:00 a.m., or on days off. However, women aged 18 years or more may consent to work during those periods if they are not pregnant or within the first year after having given birth. In addition, with approval from the MOEL after consultation with the employee representative: (i) women under 18 years old or within the first year after having given birth may consent to work during those periods; and (ii) pregnant women may work during those periods if they make a request to do so.[91] As opposed to night and day-off work, however, pregnant women may not work overtime under virtually any circumstances, and they must be assigned to light work upon request.[92]

Pregnant employees also have the right to work reduced hours. Women who are not more than twelve full weeks pregnant, or who are more than thirty-six weeks pregnant, are entitled to have their working hours reduced by up to two hours per day, but not below six hours.[93] The employer is not allowed to reduce wages due to the reduced working hours.[94] Effective 19 November 2021, pregnant employees also have the right to request changes to their starting and finishing times while maintaining their overall daily contractual working hours. An employer must accept such a request unless it causes a serious impediment to the business.[95]

A female employee may not, within the first year after childbirth, work more than two overtime hours per day, six overtime hours per week, and one hundred fifty overtime hours per year.[96]

87. LSA Art. 64(1).
88. LSA Art. 66.
89. LSA Art. 67(2).
90. LSA Art. 69.
91. LSA Art. 70.
92. LSA Art. 74(5).
93. LSA Art. 74(7).
94. LSA Art. 74(8).
95. LSA Art. 74(9).
96. LSA Art. 71.

And minors, pregnant women, and mothers within a year after childbirth are prohibited from engaging in certain hazardous or dangerous types of work designated by regulation.[97]

Women who are not on maternity leave, and who have infants under 12 months old, are permitted to take paid nursing breaks twice per day for at least thirty minutes.[98]

Employers who operate a place of business over a certain size are required to provide childcare facilities for their employees.[99]

9.9. Record-Keeping Requirements

As a general matter, irrespective of Korea's specific legally mandated record-keeping requirements, employers should keep thorough records on every important aspect of an employment relationship. In any legal proceeding for wrongful termination or improper disciplinary action, the employer bears the burden of proof, so a lack of sufficiently detailed records can be fatal to the employer's case.

9.9.1. Information That Must Be Maintained

Employers must maintain a registry that includes statutorily enumerated information about each employee who has been employed for thirty days or more.[100]

A wage ledger (payroll) must also be maintained for each workplace, and it must contain specific items of wage and hours information with respect to each employee, though certain items may be omitted for employees who have worked for fewer than thirty days, and other items may be omitted by employers with fewer than five employees or with respect to employees engaged in certain industries.[101] A ledger of grievances brought under the EEA must also be maintained.[102]

9.9.2. Records That Must Be Retained

The LSA mandates that employers preserve most documentation relating to an employment relationship, including information in the employee registry

97. LSA Art. 65(1).
98. LSA Art. 75.
99. Infant Care Act Art. 14(1).
100. LSA Art. 41, LSA Enforcement Decree Arts 20 & 21.
101. LSA Art. 48(1), LSA Enforcement Decree Art. 27(1)–(3).
102. EEA Art. 33, EEA Enforcement Decree Art. 18(3).

and wage ledger; employment contracts and other documentation of hiring, dismissal, promotion, leave, compensation changes, and other employment-related events; working-hours agreements, and employment certificates for minors. This information must be preserved for three years from the date of the relevant document or event, or the date the relevant employee ceases to be an employee, depending on its type.[103]

The EEA also requires that employers preserve for three years grievance reports, documentation respecting employment information for non-discrimination purposes, mandatory sexual-harassment-prevention education and disciplinary measures against harassers, paternity leave, and childcare leave and working hours' reductions.[104]

An employer must also preserve any material documents regarding industrial accident compensation until the relevant claim for compensation is satisfied or discharged or the statute of limitations for a claim for compensation (i.e., three years) expires.[105]

And an employer must keep records collected for its employees' year-end tax adjustment, for five years from the tax return due date.[106]

The results of mandatory employee medical examinations must be preserved for a five-year retention period.[107] However, if the examination is of employees who are engaged in handling substances designated and enumerated by the MOEL, the records must be kept for thirty years.[108]

9.9.3. Failure to Maintain Required Records

Failure to comply with these record-keeping requirements can result in an administrative fine of up to KRW 5 million (KRW 3 million for the EEA and OSHA).[109]

9.10. Reductions in Compensation Caused by Economic Downturn

Unlike layoffs, which are governed by Article 24 of the LSA, there are no statutory guidelines to follow for reducing wages for business reasons. However, if a business is suspended during a period of economic hardship, or workers are otherwise furloughed due to a sufficient cause which is

103. LSA Art. 42, LSA Enforcement Decree Art. 22.
104. EEA Art. 33, EEA Enforcement Decree Arts 18(3) & 19.
105. LSA Arts 91–92.
106. Framework Act on National Taxes 85-3.
107. OSHA Art. 164(1), OSHA Enforcement Regulation Art. 241(2).
108. OSHA Enforcement Regulation Art. 241(2).
109. LSA Art. 116(2)(2), EEA Art. 39(4)(8), OSHA Art. 175(6)(18).

attributable to the employer, the employer may reduce employees' pay to 70% of their average wages or 100% of their ordinary wages, whichever is lower, or to an even lesser amount with permission from the Labor Relations Commission.[110]

9.11. Checklist of Do's and Don'ts

- Institute an accurate system for tracking the hours of non-exempt employees and correctly managing their pay for overtime and night time work, and work during days off. Do not assume that because a category of employee is exempt in another jurisdiction, that category is also exempt in Korea. Do not simply rely on a contractual agreement to exclude an otherwise non-exempt employee from applicable overtime rules.
- Evaluate the wage system to determine which items are or are not included in employees' ordinary wages (i.e., regular, uniform, predetermined payments, as discussed in section 5.2), so as to accurately determine their entitlement to overtime, night time, and day-off pay.
- Pay all compensation and benefits no later than fourteen days from the date of an employee's departure.
- Do not apply any deductions to an employee's compensation other than those specifically authorized by statute or CBA, or pursuant to the advice of legal counsel, even where the setoff is for an indisputable debt.
- Ensure that all required records are created and preserved for at least three years. However, the requisite records and minimum preservation period are minimums, subject to applicable privacy laws that may require the disposal of non-mandatory employee records (*see* section 16.1). Bear in mind that an employer will have the burden of proof in many common legal disputes with its employees.

10. OTHER WORKING CONDITIONS AND BENEFITS: BY STATUTE, COLLECTIVE AGREEMENTS OR COMPANY POLICY

10.1. Health and Other Insurance

Korea has a national health insurance programme regulated by the National Health Insurance Act (NHIA), in which virtually all employees must be enrolled.[111] Premiums are a capped percentage of remuneration – subject to

110. LSA Art. 46.
111. NHIA Arts 5 & 109(2), NHIA Enforcement Decree Art. 76(1). Part-time workers contracted for fewer than sixty hours per month, for example, may be excluded. NHIA Art. 6(2)(4), NHIA Enforcement Decree Art. 9.

deductions and exemptions – as set by regulation within statutory limits. The premium is annually adjusted, and the rate is currently 7.09% of remuneration, an increase of 0.1% from the previous year.[112] Monthly remuneration is usually calculated based on the previous year's total remuneration, where possible.[113] The obligation to pay the required premium is split 50/50 between employee and employer, with the employer required to deduct the necessary amount from each employee's pay. Employees who earn more than a certain income threshold other than salary income are liable for additional premium amounts but without any further employer contribution.

Virtually all enrollees in Korea's national health insurance must also pay long-term-care insurance premiums in accordance with the Act on Long-Term-Care Insurance for the Aged (LTCIA). The premiums are a fixed percentage of the national health insurance premiums (currently 12.81%) imposed on each of the employee's and employer's shares.[114]

Most employees are also mandatorily enrolled in Korea's employment insurance programme,[115] which is governed by the Employment Insurance Act (EIA) and the Act on the Collection of Premiums for Employment Insurance and Industrial Accident Compensation Insurance (the 'Collection Act').[116] The employment insurance programme consists of two components: (i) unemployment benefits; and (ii) employment security and vocational skills development projects. The scope of the employment insurance programme has gradually expanded to protect various types of freelancers and similar workers. Since December 2020, it has expanded several times to protect various types of workers, such as freelance artists, insurance agents, freelance instructors, IT software engineers and those who provide certain platform-based services such as certain delivery workers, quick service drivers and designated drivers, home appliance delivery installers, freight drivers, and golf course caddies.[117]

Premiums for unemployment benefits are paid half each by the employer and employee. However, employment security and vocational skills development projects are funded entirely by employer contributions. The employee contributions are withheld by the employer.

---

112. Notification of Increase in the National Health Insurance (NHI) Contribution from 2023. Available in Korean and English at the NHIS website (nhis.or.kr).
113. NHIA Enforcement Decree Arts 34 & 36.
114. LTCIA Arts 7–9.
115. EIA Art. 77-6, EIA Enforcement Decree Art. 104-11.
116. EIA Art. 8, Collection Act Art. 5. Certain categories of business are exempt (e.g., agricultural businesses with fewer than five employees, and certain small construction projects). EIA Art. 8, EIA Enforcement Decree Art. 2(1). Certain employees are also exempt or partially exempt (e.g., employees employed after age 65, and employees who work fewer than sixty hours per month or fifteen hours per week – with limitations – are exempt from the unemployment insurance portion). EIA Art. 10, EIA Enforcement Decree Art. 3.
117. EIA Art. 77-6, EIA Enforcement Decree Art. 104-11.

10.2. Pension and Retirement Benefits

Under Korea's National Pension Act (NPA), virtually all employees between 18 and 60 years old are required to be enrolled in the national pension system, with employer and employee each responsible for half of the premium.[118] The total premium is 9% of earned income, subject to reduction to the extent of certain tax-deductible income, and subject to a cap that is adjusted each year in July.[119] Premiums must be withheld from employees' wages and paid by the employer.

All employees who serve at least one year, and work an average of fifteen or more weekly hours per four-week period, are also entitled to retirement (or severance) benefits under the ERBSA, unless they work in a business employing only relatives living together.[120] Although domestic/household employees were not previously entitled to such benefits, such employees became entitled as of 16 June 2022, subject to certain requirements.[121] To this end, employers are required to provide one of the following: (i) a defined-benefit pension plan capable of paying thirty days or more of an employee's average wages, for each year of consecutive service; (ii) a defined-contribution retirement plan to which the employer contributes an amount equal to at least one-twelfth of an employee's annual compensation;[122] or (iii) simple payment of thirty days or more of an employee's average wages for each year of consecutive service.[123] If no plan is set up, the employer is deemed to have opted for the last option and is required to pay thirty days' average wages for each year of consecutive service. Payment of benefits to eligible recipients, or transfer of retirement funds, must be effected within fourteen days of termination to avoid the risk of criminal liability.[124]

Effective 12 July 2022, severance pension trustees are required to implement one or more 'default option schemes,' which are certain kinds of low-risk pension-fund investment products/plans that will apply if a defined-contribution pension-plan subscriber fails to choose any financial

118. NPA Arts 6, 8(1) & 126. Employees under 18 may request enrolment. NPA Art. 8(2).
119. NPA Art. 88, NPA Enforcement Decree Arts 3 & 5.
120. ERBSA Arts 3 & 4(1).
121. Act on the Employment Improvement of Family Workers Art. 6(1).
122. Effective 14 Apr. 2022, the Small and Medium-sized Enterprise (SME) Retirement Pension Fund Plan (SME Plan) was implemented for SMEs with thirty or fewer full-time employees (ERBSA Art. 23-2). The SME Plan is intended to provide retirement benefits to employees through the establishment and operation of a joint fund with contributions paid by multiple SME employers and their employees. The SME Plan contribution requirement is calculated in the same manner as a defined-contribution retirement plan. However, the two differ in that, while defined-contribution pension plans require employees to directly manage their funds, the SME Plan entrusts the Workers' Compensation & Welfare Service and other outside professional organizations.
123. ERBSA Arts 8, 15 & 20.
124. ERBSA Arts 9, 17(2)–(5), 20(5) & 44.

product/strategy to manage their account funds; the default option scheme must be approved by the MOEL and also presented to the employer so it can seek consent from an employee representative.[125]

Establishing a new type of plan or changing from one type to another requires consent from a majority union or a majority of employees if there is no such union, as do adverse changes to the details of the plan. However, the law instructs employers formed after 25 July 2012 to create either a defined-benefit or defined-contribution plan within a year of their establishment, after consultation with employees but with no requirement to obtain consent.

10.3. Vacation and Holiday, and Related Payments on Termination

Part-time employees whose contractual working hours average fewer than fifteen hours per week over a four-week period (or their period of employment, during the first four weeks) are not entitled to any weekly days off or annual leave.[126]

Other employees are entitled to an average of one paid day off per week in which they have perfect attendance.[127] Although employers usually give their employees both Sunday and Saturday off, they may designate only one day as a paid day off, and the other as unpaid.

And employers with five or more employees must provide them with statutory paid annual leave.[128] Employees must receive fifteen days of paid annual leave immediately after each of their first year and second year of service (if they attend work for 80% of the year). Their yearly leave accrual increases to sixteen days after the third year, and every two years thereafter, increases by another one day, up to a maximum of twenty-five days per year. Employees may also, during their first year of service, take one day of leave for each month in which the employee worked without an absence, for a total of eleven days. Prior to an amendment to the law (effective 29 May 2018), any days used in this manner during the first year were deducted from the following year's leave allowance. However, the amendment disallowed the practice of deducting the monthly leave in the first year from the fifteen days of annual leave granted after the first year. This made the monthly leave in year one a distinct grant of leave rather than an advance on the fifteen-day grant of leave. After a year in which an employee fails to satisfy the 80%

125. ERBSA Arts 19(1), 21-2, 21-3 & 21-4.
126. LSA Art. 18(3).
127. LSA Arts 11(1) & 55(1), LSA Enforcement Decree Art. 7 & Table 1. Employees in certain professions are exempt from this entitlement. LSA Art. 63.
128. LSA Art. 60.

work-attendance requirement, one day per month of attendance without an absence is granted instead of the fifteen or more days granted to those who have met the 80% attendance requirement.

In late 2021, the Supreme Court held that employees whose employment terminates after *exactly* one year (i.e., those on a non-renewed one-year contract) are not entitled to compensation for the fifteen days' annual leave accrued *after* one year of service. This decision overturned the MOEL's interpretation by which employees *were* entitled to compensation for those fifteen days immediately after a one-year term of employment.[129] Furthermore, in September 2022, the Supreme Court reaffirmed its 2021 decision, explaining that an employee who has worked for fifteen months accrued eleven days of annual leave for the first year of service, and was entitled to fifteen days of annual leave on the day *following* the completion of the first year of service (the beginning of the second year of service), totalling a maximum of twenty-six days of annual leave.[130] Thus, an employee whose employment ends after *exactly* one year of service will accrue only eleven days of annual leave, while an employee whose employment ends after more than one year but less than two years of service will accrue eleven days over the first year of service and fifteen days immediately at the beginning of the second year of service, for a total of twenty-six days of annual leave.

Employees may use their annual leave upon their request and must be paid, at a minimum, their ordinary wage while on annual leave. An employee's right to annual leave expires if unused within one year unless the employer effectively prevents the employee from using it. An employer must compensate an employee for any expired, unused annual leave – however, an employer can require employees to use their annual leave by implementing a statutory procedure for encouraging the use of leave:

(i) Starting six months immediately before unused leave is to expire, the employer has ten days to notify the employee of the number of unused leave days and urge the employee in writing to decide when to use them.
(ii) If the employee does not choose when to take the unused leave within ten days of that notice, the employer must determine a leave period and notify the employee at least two months before the leave is to expire.[131]

Prior to a recent amendment to the LSA, the eleven days of leave granted monthly in the first year, and the one day per month granted to employees who fail to meet the 80% attendance requirement, could not be subject to the

129. S. Ct. Case No. 2021Da227100 (14 Oct. 2021).
130. S. Ct. Case No. 2022Da245419 (7 Sep. 2022).
131. LSA Art. 61.

leave-use-encouragement procedure described above. Thus, employees always had to be compensated for that leave if it expired. Effective from 31 March 2020, employers are able to require employees to use both the monthly (first year) and annually granted leave by using the leave-use-encouragement procedure. In the case of the eleven days of first-year leave granted monthly, the law provides a similar mechanism with adjusted dates for the notices; to allow the system to work, the new amendment also makes all of those eleven days of leave expire at the same time, one year after commencement of employment, instead of making them expire on a staggered basis one year after each day is granted, as under prior law.

Until recently, Labor Day (1 May) was the only mandatory paid national holiday for private-sector employees.[132] Eligible voters were also required to be allowed sufficient time off to vote in elections, and to fulfil other civic or official duties, during working hours,[133] and employers have often given employees election days off entirely. But public holidays generally were not *mandatory* in the private sector. The ubiquitous market practice, however, has been to provide all or almost all of the same paid days off to private-sector employees as were provided to public-sector employees. These holidays are: New Year (1 January); Lunar New Year (first day of the Lunar Calendar, plus two additional days); Independence Movement Day (1 March); Children's Day (5 May); Buddha's Birthday (eighth day of fourth Lunar month); Memorial Day (6 June); Liberation Day (15 August); Chuseok (i.e., Korean Thanksgiving, fifteenth day of fourth Lunar month, plus two additional days); National Foundation Day (3 October); Hangeul (the Korean alphabet) Day (9 October); Christmas (25 December); and election days under the Public Official Election Act.

The LSA now requires most employers to guarantee employees paid holidays as prescribed by regulation[134] which are the holidays stated above. That law was phased in by employer size and finally became effective on 1 January 2022 for employers with five or more but less than thirty employees.[135] Employers with fewer than five employees will continue to be exempt.

If any day of the Chuseok or Lunar New Year holidays falls on a Sunday or another public holiday, then the next working day will be granted as a substitute paid holiday (the same rule applies to the Independence Movement Day, Liberation Day, National Foundation Day, Hangeul (Korean

132. Act on Establishment of Labor Day.
133. LSA Art. 10.
134. LSA Art. 55(2) & LSA Presidential Decree Art. 30. When the employer makes a written agreement with the labour representative, such paid holidays may be substituted with particular working days.
135. LSA Art. 55 & Addenda of Act. No. 15513 (20 Mar. 2018) Art. 1(4).

alphabet) Day, Buddha's Birthday, Christmas or Children's Day if they fall on a Saturday or Sunday).

Compensation for accrued but unused leave must be provided within fourteen days of termination to avoid the risk of criminal liability.[136]

10.4. Leaves of Absence

10.4.1. Personal Leave

Only statutory annual leave and the specific forms of leave below are mandatory under Korean law.

10.4.2. Medical or Sick Leave

There is no general obligation for employers to provide medical or sick leave for non-work-related injuries or illnesses, although employers frequently provide for such leave in their work rules. At employers with five or more employees, however, female employees are entitled to one day of unpaid menstruation leave per month upon request.

Employers are generally liable for the treatment for workplace injuries, as discussed below in section 11.

10.4.3. Bereavement Leave

There is no requirement to provide bereavement leave to employees, although employers frequently provide for such leave in their work rules.

10.4.4. Childcare and Family Leave

An employee who has worked continuously for an employer for six months or more,[137] and who has a child (including an adopted child) aged 8 years or less or who has not yet reached the third grade of elementary school, is entitled to take childcare leave for up to one year.[138] The period of childcare leave must be treated as part of the employee's continuous service period but is not counted for purposes of determining whether a fixed-term employee or

136. LSA Arts 36 & 109(1).
137. Effective as of 18 May 2021, EEA Art. 19(1) expanded eligibility for childcare leave to include pregnant female employees.
138. EEA Art. 19.

dispatched worker becomes a permanent employee by operation of law after two years of continuous service. Under a relatively recent amendment to the EEA, an employee is now eligible to take a childcare leave even if the employee's spouse is taking childcare leave for the same child. Childcare leave may be unpaid, but an employee may be eligible for a government subsidy of a certain percentage of the employee's ordinary wage.

An employee who is eligible for childcare leave may also request a reduction in working hours to accommodate childcare responsibilities for up to two years *minus* any of the one year of available childcare *leave* that has been used by the employee – in other words, an eligible employee can take one year as reduced hours and can take another separate year as leave *or* reduced hours, *or* a combination of the two.[139] Reduced working hours can be from fifteen to thirty-five per week, with up to twelve hours of overtime at the specific request of the employee. A request for reduced hours can only be denied: (i) if the employee is ineligible; (ii) if the employer cannot find a reasonable substitute employee within fourteen days or more of listing the opening with an employment security office; or (iii) if the nature of the job makes it difficult to split up the working hours or the employer can prove that the working-hours reduction will cause serious disruption to the business.[140] The employer must provide the reasons for the denial in writing, and other measures to support childcare responsibilities must be taken instead.

If the employee would be eligible for government support during childcare leave, the employee will be eligible for a government subsidy during a period of reduced hours for childcare.[141]

An employee's one year of childcare leave per child may be used as either one or two separate periods of leave (not counting any periods used during pregnancy) which, combined, equals no more than one year in total; whereas reduced hours for childcare may be split into multiple uses of at least three continuous months each.[142]

Employees who have worked for an employer for at least six months are entitled to up to ninety days of leave per year, if needed for the care of a sick, elderly, or injured parent, child, spouse, spouse's parent and, as of 1 January 2020, grandparent or grandchild.[143] The leave may be taken in separate periods of as few as thirty days each. However, as of 1 January 2020, ten days can be used individually to care for family members as provided above, or for 'taking care of children' (e.g., attending school events). An employer need not grant such family-care leave: (i) if another family member is able

139. EEA Art. 19-2.
140. EEA Enforcement Decree Art. 15(2) & 15-2.
141. EIA Art. 73-2(1).
142. EEA Arts 19, 19-2 & 19-4.
143. EEA Art. 22-2.

to provide the necessary care; (ii) if the employer cannot find a reasonable substitute employee within fourteen days or more of listing the opening with an employment security office; or (iii) if the employer proves that the leave will cause serious business disruption. The employer must follow a similar procedure for a denial of reduced hours for childcare.

The option to take reduced hours for family care was introduced under a phase-in schedule. The last phase-in group, employers with fewer than thirty employees, became subject as of 1 January 2021. Reduced working hours must be no less than fifteen hours and no more than thirty hours per week,[144] and the reduced-hours period must not exceed one year in total.

10.4.5. Pregnancy and Maternity Leave

In addition to the pre-natal and post-natal maternity leave discussed below, employers with five or more employees must allow pregnant female employees to take time off for regular pre-natal medical examinations, and their wages may not be cut for making use of that time off.[145]

All female employees must be granted at least ninety days of pre- and post-natal maternity leave, of which at least forty-five days must be post-natal.[146] For women pregnant with two or more children, one hundred twenty days of maternity leave must be granted, of which sixty days must be post-natal.[147] Employees who have previously had a miscarriage or stillbirth, who are 40 or more years old, or who provide a doctor's opinion that they have a high risk of miscarriage or stillbirth may take the pre-natal portion of their maternity leave in non-consecutive periods.[148]

A woman who experiences a miscarriage or stillbirth is entitled to an amount of leave based on the duration of the pregnancy, ranging from five days of leave after no more than eleven full weeks of pregnancy, to a maximum of ninety days after twenty-eight weeks of pregnancy.[149] The leave period is measured from the date of the miscarriage or stillbirth.[150]

The first sixty days – seventy-five days for women pregnant with two or more children – of the employee's maternity, stillbirth, or miscarriage leave must be paid, and with respect to employees who have worked one hundred eighty days or more, the government's employment insurance programme will pay the employee's ordinary wage – up to a cap – for the remaining days. However, if the employer has less than a certain number of employees,

144. EEA Art. 22-3.
145. LSA Art. 74-2.
146. LSA Art. 74(1).
147. LSA Art. 74(1).
148. LSA Art. 74(2).
149. LSA Art. 74(3), LSA Enforcement Decree Art. 43(3).
150. LSA Enforcement Decree Art. 43(3).

based on industry, the government will pay the employee's ordinary wage – up to the cap – for the entire period.[151] The employer is then responsible only for making up the difference – if any – between that capped amount and the employer's obligation for the first sixty or seventy-five days.[152]

A male employee is entitled to paid paternity leave of ten paid days upon request, during the ninety days after his spouse gives birth. Paternity leave can be split and used in two separate leave periods.[153]

10.4.6. Injury at Work

See section 11.

10.5. Checklist of Do's and Don'ts

- Encourage employees to use their annual leave by means of the statutorily prescribed methods described above in section 10.3 so as to ensure adequate rest and avoid paying compensation for unused leave.
- Employers that qualify for support because they have fewer than a certain number of employees, as described above in section 10.4, should facilitate their eligible employees' application for government support during maternity leave, and leave for miscarriage or stillbirth. These government benefits may reduce the employer's obligation to pay compensation for the leave period. Employers should also evaluate whether they qualify for government subsidies.

11. INDUSTRIAL ACCIDENT COMPENSATION (WORKERS' COMPENSATION)

11.1. Overview

Chapter VIII of the LSA places the responsibility to pay for the treatment of workplace injuries and illnesses on employers, without requiring any finding of fault. It also provides employees with a right to continue receiving a percentage of their compensation while undergoing treatment for such injury or illness, as well as further compensation if they remain disabled after treatment unless the employer proves to the Labor Relations Commission that the injury, illness, or disability was caused by the employee's gross

151. EIA Arts 75 & 76(1)–(2), EIA Enforcement Decree Art. 12.
152. EEA Art. 18(2), LSA Art. 74(4).
153. EEA Art. 18-2.

negligence. Death benefits are also required to be paid if an employee dies on the job.

A primary contractor is liable for these forms of accident and illness compensation, with respect to its subcontractor's employees.

However, Korea also has a mandatory workers' compensation insurance scheme in which most employers and employees must be enrolled. Employers are relieved of responsibility for the compensation described above, to the extent that equivalent benefits are paid under the workers' compensation insurance scheme.

11.2. The Industrial Accident Compensation Insurance Act

Korea's Industrial Accident Compensation Insurance Act (IACIA), together with the Collection Act, requires almost all employers to enroll their employees in the state's industrial accident compensation insurance scheme, with the Korea Workers' Compensation and Welfare Service paying insurance benefits to employees who suffer an industrial accident or illness. Effective as of 1 January 2022, the industrial accident compensation insurance scheme also applies to students who participate in research and development projects at universities and research institutes.[154] The industrial accident compensation scheme covers workers who are not 'employees' under the LSA but are engaged in certain defined jobs where they provide 'employee-like' labour, known as 'persons in special types of employment.' This category includes, for example, many delivery people, for-hire designated drivers, home-visit maintenance engineers, and online platform workers. Persons in special types of employment currently must work for only one business to be covered by the IACIA, but the IACIA's 'exclusivity' requirement will be revoked effective 1 July 2023 so that such workers can be covered even if they provide services to multiple businesses.[155]

The IACIA applies to all employers, with limited exceptions applicable to employees covered by other schemes (such as teachers, public officials, and members of the military); household employees; and employers in the agricultural, forestry, fishing, and hunting businesses with fewer than five employees.[156] Effective as of 12 January 2023, industrial accident compensation insurance will cover a pregnant employee's newborn child who suffers from an injury, illness, or disability, or who dies, due to an industrial accident involving the employee-mother, or from an accident

154. IACIA Art 123-2, Collection Act Art. 48-5.
155. IACIA Art. 91-15–91-21.
156. IACIA Art. 6.

during commuting to or from work, or from handling of or exposure to harmful factors in the course of performing her duties.[157]

Insurance premiums are payable entirely by employers in general, but employers and employees engaged in special types of employment (referred to above in this section) will each bear 50% of the premiums for industrial accident compensation insurance. Nonetheless, in some cases the employer will bear the full amount of the insurance premiums in consideration of the subordinate relationship between such employer and employee.[158]

Unlike in some other jurisdictions, an entitlement to workers' compensation insurance is not a bar to obtaining civil damages for workplace injuries sustained due to an employer's fault. Instead, benefits received under the IACIA provide a set off against any compensation for the same injury from another source, including the employer's liability for workers' compensation under the LSA, as well as civil tort damages.

11.3. Criteria for Recognition of Work-Related Accidents

The IACIA covers only work-related accidents and illnesses. Article 37 of the IACIA defines the following enumerated kinds of accidents and illnesses as 'work related'.

11.3.1. Work-Related Accidents

(i) An accident that happens while the employee is performing the employee's work or another act in accordance with the employee's employment contract.
(ii) An accident that happens due to a defect in, or the careless management of, facilities provided by the employer while the employee is using these facilities.
(iii) An accident that happens while the employee is participating in or preparing an event organized by the employer or an event following the directions of the employer.
(iv) An accident that happens during recess hours due to an act that occurs under the control of the employer.
(v) Other accidents which happen in relation to the employee's work.

157. IACIA Art. 91-12–91-14.
158. Collection Act Art. 48-6.

11.3.2. Work-Related Illnesses

(i) An illness that occurs due to the handling of, or exposure to, harmful or hazardous materials while the employee is performing the employee's duties.
(ii) An illness which occurs as a result of a work-related injury.
(iii) Mental distress caused by workplace bullying and harassment, including verbal abuse by a client or customer.[159]
(iv) Other illnesses which occur in relation to the employee's work.

However, if there is no proximate causal relationship between an employee's duties and the accident or illness, it is not considered work-related even if it otherwise satisfies Article 37. Also, injury, disease, disability, or death resulting from an employee's intentional act, self-injury, or criminal conduct is not considered work related.

11.3.3. Commuting Accidents

(i) An accident that happens while the employee is commuting to and from work under the control of the employer, such as using transportation provided by the employer or the equivalent thereof.
(ii) Other accidents during commuting with usual routes and methods.[160]

11.4. Types of Workers' Compensation Insurance Benefits

The following kinds of benefits are provided under the IACIA.

159. This form of 'work-related illness' became part of the law effective 16 Jul. 2019, by an amendment to the Industrial Accident Compensation Insurance Act that references the workplace harassment newly defined by an amendment to the LSA effective 16 Jul. 2019.

160. Accidents occurring during an interruption of or departure from the commuting route will not constitute commuting accidents under this provision; provided, however, when such interruption or departure is necessary and has a reason prescribed by Presidential Decree, then such accidents will constitute commuting accidents under this provision. For certain occupations, where the route and method of commuting is not constant, this provision regarding commuting accidents will not be applicable.

11.4.1. Medical Care Benefits

Medical care benefits for an injury or disease that requires medical care for more than three days (i.e., that cannot be resolved by treatment within three days or less), including for any recurrence.[161]

11.4.2. Wage Replacement Benefits

Wage replacement benefits are paid to any employee who suffers an occupational injury or illness, for the period during which the employee is unable to work in order to receive medical care.[162] The daily amount of wage replacement benefits is 70% of the employee's average wage. Special provisions adjust this entitlement with respect to low-income employees, elderly employees, and employees who work during a portion of their treatment period. Like medical care benefits themselves, wage replacement benefits are not payable if the care period is three days or less.

11.4.3. Disability Benefits

A worker who suffers a continuing disability resulting from a work-related injury or illness even after receiving medical care is eligible to receive disability benefits.[163] Disability benefits consist of a disability compensation annuity or lump-sum disability compensation, according to a disability grading system using fourteen grades. The amount of disability benefits are calculated based on the employee's average wage. The disability compensation annuity ranges from 138 days' average wages for a grade seven disability up to 329 days' average wage for a grade one disability. Lump-sum disability compensation benefits range between 55 days' average wage for a grade fourteen disability and 1,474 days' average wage for a grade one disability.

11.4.4. Nursing Benefits

Nursing benefits are paid to an employee who requires constant or frequent nursing care, even after medical treatment.[164]

161. IACIA Art. 40.
162. IACIA Arts 52–56.
163. IACIA Arts 57–60 & Table 2.
164. IACIA Art. 61.

11.4.5. Survivors' Benefits and Funeral Expenses

Survivors' benefits are paid to surviving family members of an employee who has died due to work-related causes.[165] Survivors' benefits are paid in the form of a survivors' compensation annuity or lump-sum survivors' compensation. The amount of lump-sum survivors' compensation is one thousand three hundred days' average wage.

Funeral expenses are paid in the form of lump-sum survivors' compensation. The amount is one hundred and twenty days' average wage.

11.5. Checklist of Do's and Don'ts

- Most employers must enroll in and maintain industrial accident compensation insurance.
- The premiums for industrial accident compensation insurance are borne by the employer –except for certain 'persons engaged in special types of employment' as discussed in section 11.2 – and cannot be deducted from employees' compensation.

12. COMPANY'S OBLIGATION TO PROVIDE SAFE AND HEALTHY WORKPLACE

12.1. Overview of Safety and Environmental Laws and Regulations

The Occupational Safety and Health Act (OSHA) was enacted in 1981 to maintain and promote the safety and health of workers by establishing standards on industrial health and safety, clarifying the responsibilities of employers and employees and promoting healthy working environments. The OSHA applies to all employers. However, certain categories of employer are exempt from certain of its provisions, respectively, as prescribed by regulation; for example, the provisions described below requiring the appointment of safety managers and the preparation of health-and-safety regulations are not applicable to employers in many industries, and employers with fewer than five full-time employees.

On 15 January 2019, the OSHA was significantly amended. This is the most extensive amendment to the OSHA since its initial passage in 1990. Most significantly, the bill expands its protections to more broadly cover workers who are not direct employees, strengthens businesses' responsibility to prevent industrial accidents, and imposes new disclosure requirements for

165. IACIA Arts 62–65, 71 & Table 3.

manufacturers and importers of dangerous chemicals, among other things. The amendment is effective as of 16 January 2020.

12.2. Safety-and-Health Management System

The MOEL may subject a workplace to a health-and-safety inspection conducted by a health-and-safety inspection institution. The employee representative must be allowed to attend any such health-and-safety inspection.[166] The OSHA requires companies of a certain scale and type of business to appoint various health-and-safety management personnel – discussed in more detail below – in order to establish and manage their own health-and-safety systems.

An employer is also responsible for taking measures to prevent industrial accidents which may occur for its employees and those employed by a third-party contractor who work at the employer's workplace.[167]

12.3. Duties of Employer

The following duties are imposed on all employers, except that employers may be exempt from one or more requirements by having fewer than five employees, using only white-collar employees, or falling within certain categories of business.

12.3.1. Appointment of Health-and-Safety Manager

The OSHA requires employers to appoint various officers in charge of health-and-safety functions, depending on the size and industry of the employer. These positions include a health-and-safety manager, with broad responsibility for general oversight and management of health-and-safety matters, as well as a variety of subordinate and ancillary health-and-safety positions, and a health-and-safety committee.[168]

Companies that are sufficiently small are permitted to outsource some of these functions to a MOEL-approved service provider. If an employer fails

166. OSHA Art. 47.

167. OSHA Art. 63. The employer's workplace includes a workplace listed in the Enforcement Decree of the OSHA that an employer provided or designated.

168. Starting from 1 Sep. 2019, a certain requirement to appoint a health-and-safety manager that had applied to manufacturing employers with thirty or more but fewer than fifty employees was expanded to also cover employers with twenty to twenty-nine employees. OSHA Art. 19, OSHA Enforcement Decree Art. 24.

to comply with these requirements, an administrative fine of up to KRW 5 million may be imposed.

12.3.2. Preparation of Health-and-Safety Policies

Non-exempt employers must prepare health-and-safety policies that meet certain minimum statutory requirements, post or keep them in the workplace, and notify their employees thereof. The applicability of this requirement depends on the nature and size of the business, but generally employers with fewer than one hundred employees are exempt. Health-and-safety policies must not be contrary to the employer's CBA, if any, and its rules of employment.[169] If an employer fails to comply with these requirements, it is an offence punishable by an administrative fine of up to KRW 5 million. Most employers are required to post a description of the major requirements of the OSHA or otherwise make it available at the workplace.[170]

12.3.3. Measures for Preventing Harm and Hazards

The OSHA requires that employers: (i) instal or attach health-and-safety-related signs to warn employees of harmful or dangerous facilities and locations in the workplace, to provide measures for dealing with potential emergencies, and to promote safety awareness; (ii) take safety measures necessary for the prevention of hazards caused by dangerous equipment; (iii) take measures to prevent health problems caused by gases, powder, or excessive physical labour; (iv) take measures, such as providing instructions and a manual to prevent employees from being abused or assaulted by customers; and (v) where there exists an imminent danger that an industrial accident may occur, or a serious accident has occurred, the employer must take necessary health-and-safety measures, such as the immediate suspension of operations and evacuation of workers from the workplace. Under the OSHA amendment effective 16 January 2020, if an employee believes that there exists an imminent danger of an industrial accident, that employee may cease work and cannot be dismissed or punished if he or she had a reasonable reason to believe that there was an imminent danger of an industrial accident.

169. OSHA Art. 25.
170. OSHA Art. 34.

12.4. Duties of a Representative Director

The representative director of a company with 500 or more employees (or a construction company publicized to be within the top 1,000 in construction capability) must develop a safety-and-health plan to report to the board of directors for approval. Failure to comply with this duty can result in an administrative fine of up to KRW 10 million.

12.5. Management of Employee Health

12.5.1. Working Environment Assessment

Employers must conduct tests to assess the safety of work environments where work that is potentially harmful to the health and safety of employees is carried out, as prescribed by regulation of the MOEL.[171] Failure to comply with the testing requirement can result in an administrative fine of up to KRW 10 million. Employers must take appropriate measures to protect the health of employees, including installation and improvement of facilities and equipment, in accordance with the results of these tests.[172] Subsequent to conducting such tests, failure to take corrective measures to protect workers' health may result in a fine of up to KRW 10 million.

Effective from 18 August 2022, for employers with fifty or more employees, and from 18 August 2023, for employers with twenty or more employees *or ten or more employees of whom* at least two are in enumerated types of (riskier) work (*these thresholds also include contractors' employees), an administrative* fine of up to KRW 15 million may be imposed for failure to instal rest facilities when required under the OSHA.[173] And an administrative fine of up to KRW 10 million may be imposed for failure to comply with the specific rest-facility standards required under the OSHA, where applicable, such as those related to size, location, temperature and lighting.[174] Employers who do not meet these workforce-size thresholds are technically also obligated to have rest facilities, but they are not subject to any specific rest-facility standards. Additionally, according to the MOEL's guidelines, a workplace with only office workers, who can rest free of work-related interruptions during their breaks, is not subject to the rest-facility requirements.

171. OSHA Art. 125(1).
172. OSHA Art. 125(6).
173. OSHA Art. 128-2(1) & OSHA Art. 175(3).
174. OSHA Art. 128-2(2) & OSHA Art. 175(4).

12.5.2. Medical Examinations

Employers must conduct one or more of various kinds of health examinations of their employees, including general health examinations,[175] pre-placement medical examinations, special medical examinations, and immediate health examinations, as provided by regulation of the MOEL. Employees must undergo these mandatory health examinations provided by their employers. However, if any employee does not want to receive a health examination by an institution designated by the employer, the employee may take an equivalent health examination conducted by another health examination institution. An employer who does not conduct the required health examinations is subject to an administrative fine of up to KRW 10 million. These examinations can be procured through approved third-party service providers.

An institution that has conducted the required health examination must notify the employer of the results to the extent required to address any workplace illnesses, and the employer may be required to take measures to protect the health and safety of employees in light of the results of their health examinations, such as transfers, shortened working hours, and installation or improvement of facilities and equipment. Failure to comply with the requirement to take such measures can result in a fine of up to KRW 10 million. The employer may not disclose the results of the health examinations of its employees without their consent, nor use such results for any purpose other than the purpose of protecting and maintaining the health of employees. If the employer fails to comply with these requirements, an administrative fine of up to KRW 5 million (or KRW 3 million for abusing the results) may be imposed.

12.5.3. Prohibition of Dangerous Work

An employer must prohibit or restrict the work of individuals suffering from communicable diseases or mental illness, or a sickness that might worsen due to the employee's work and that is prescribed by regulation of the MOEL (e.g., schizophrenia, dementia paralytica), in accordance with the diagnosis of a doctor, and must promptly permit the affected employee to resume work upon regaining proper health.[176] If the employer fails to

175. A general health examination refers to a health examination regularly conducted for full-time employees. General health examinations must be conducted once every two years or more for office employees and once a year or more for other kinds of employees. OSHA Enforcement Regulation Art. 197.

176. OSHA Art. 138(1)–(2).

comply with these requirements, a fine of up to KRW 10 million may be imposed.

For harmful or dangerous work prescribed by regulation of the MOEL, an employer must not permit any person to perform it other than those who have the qualifications, license, experience, or skill required to do so.[177] Any breach of this requirement may result in imprisonment for up to three years or a fine of up to KRW 30 million. An employer may not cause an employee who is engaged in harmful or dangerous work involving the use of a caisson or which is otherwise performed under high barometric pressure, to work in excess of six hours per day or thirty-four hours per week.[178] Other forms of hazardous work enumerated by government regulation also require extra attention to working hours, though without being subject to the same firm limit. Failure to comply with this requirement may result in a penalty of imprisonment for no more than three years or a fine of up to KRW 30 million.

Effective as of 16 January 2020, the OSHA prohibits the contracting out or outsourcing of the following types of work: plating, refining, casting, and heating mercury, lead, and cadmium. The amendment, however, provides exceptions: temporary and intermittent work can be outsourced, as well as outsourcing work that is inevitable for the business to a contractor who has professional skills.[179]

12.6. Fines and Penalties

In addition to the penalties listed above, the OSHA imposes joint penal liability on a corporation or individual whose agent or employee commits an offence in connection with the business of the corporation or individual, unless reasonably diligent supervision is exercised.

Effective from 16 January 2020, the amended OSHA now imposes penalties not only with respect to one's own *employees* but also when a business's failure to take the required safety-and-health measures with respect to the workers of its *contractors* leads to death, and there are elevated penalties for repeated fatal accidents due to the same cause. Recently, the Supreme Court found a representative director of a ship-building business guilty of negligence after the death of the contractor's workers, based on the representative director's duty to take required safety-and-health measures with respect to the contractors' employees.[180]

177. OSHA Art. 140(1).
178. OSHA Art. 139(1), OSHA Enforcement Decree Art. 99.
179. OSHA Art. 58.
180. S. Ct. Case No. 2020Do15325 (27 Oct. 2022).

12.7. Penalties for Severe Accidents

Recently, the Korean National Assembly passed the controversial Severe Accidents Penalties Act (SAPA), which establishes new health-and-safety obligations for businesses and their executives, particularly CEOs, and imposes serious penalties on those businesses and the responsible executives where failure to fulfil those obligations results in death, or in serious injuries or illnesses that satisfy certain thresholds.

SAPA is effective as of 27 January 2022. However, the provisions of SAPA concerning industrial accidents will not apply to employers with fewer than fifty employees (or construction businesses involving projects that cost less than KRW 5 billion) until 26 January 2024.

The core responsibilities imposed on 'responsible executives' by SAPA are: (1) establishing and implementing a safety-and-health management system with the personnel and budget necessary to prevent accidents; (2) if an accident occurs, establishing and implementing measures to prevent its reoccurrence; (3) taking measures to comply with any corrective orders by national or local governments agencies, in accordance with relevant laws and regulations; and (4) taking measures necessary to ensure that obligations under other safety-and-health-related laws and regulations are met.[181] The enforcement decree of SAPA provides more specific details of the above responsibilities to a certain degree, but much still remains uncertain despite the issuance of MOEL guidelines. This uncertainty may be somewhat addressed by pending court decisions – more than ten relevant cases are pending in court as of the time of this writing.

12.8. Checklists of Do's and Don'ts

– An employer should carefully evaluate which provisions of the OSHA apply to it and to its employees because the applicable provisions vary based on the size of the business and its activities.
– Non-exempt employers must appoint a person in charge of safety-and-health management, and other required health-and-safety officers and ancillary positions, as required for the particular workplace.
– Subject employers must prepare health-and-safety management regulations and post them or make them available in the workplace. They must also post or make available at the workplace a description of the major requirements of the OSHA.

181. SAPA Art. 4.

- Employers must take all required health-and-safety measures, and where required, they must measure the working environment for hazardous materials.
- Employers should determine the health check-ups they must provide (frequency and type) to their employees under the OSHA, and its associated regulations.
- Employers and responsible executives should comply with the requirements of SAPA and be aware of court precedents that may offer more detail regarding their responsibilities.

13. IMMIGRATION, SECONDMENT, AND FOREIGN ASSIGNMENT

13.1. Overview Laws Controlling Immigration

In Korea, there are two primary statutes regulating the employment of foreign workers. The first is the Immigration Act (IA), which regulates entry into the country and the permissible activities of foreigners generally, and sets out the requirements for and rights under various visas, some of which enable limited or unlimited employment activities. Visas permitting work activities include those for certain skilled and technical workers,[182] as well as various other types of visas under which employment activity is allowed, such as for those married to a Korean national.[183] The second statute is the Foreign Workers Employment Act (FWA), which imposes a number of additional requirements on the employment of foreign workers. However, the FWA exempts from its application the holders of a variety of visas relating to employment in technical or specialized fields, as well as non-work visas that enable employment activities, such as marriage visas. Thus the FWA generally applies to non-specialized workers who do not fall within any of those categories.

182. There are several types of visas available for the purpose of bringing skilled and technical foreign workers into Korea under the IA, which vary according to the nature of the employment activities and include: Professor (E-1), Language Instruction (E-2), Research (E-3), Technical Guidance (E-4), Expert (certain licensed professionals such as attorneys and accountants) (E-5), Art & Entertainment (E-6), and Special Activities (E-7).

183. Visas with which a foreigner may engage in employment activity in Korea, other than those granted for unskilled, skilled, and technical foreign workers generally, include: Short-Term Employment (C-4), Ethnic Korean Foreign Nationals (F-4), Permanent Residence (F-5), Marriage to Korean National (F-6), Working Holiday (H-1), Residence (F-2), and Student (D-2).

13.2. Recruiting, Screening and Hiring Process

Employers must obtain an employment permit in order to hire foreign workers under the FWA. To obtain an employment permit, an employer must have attempted and failed to hire a native Korean worker for at least fourteen days after submitting an application to an employment security office.[184] The employer is then permitted to request an employment permit for a foreign worker, whom it must select from among a list of qualified candidates supplied by the employment security office, which keeps a roster of foreign workers seeking employment in Korea. After entering into an employment contract with a selected foreign worker, the employer can apply for a work visa issuance certificate on the employee's behalf.

A foreign worker hired in this manner may work as an employee for three years upon entry into Korea.[185] This period may be extended once, for an additional period of less than two years.[186]

For specialized workers who are exempt from the FWA, the requirements for a visa application under the IA vary according to the type of visa sought. However, generally various forms of documentation, including the proposed employment contract, must be submitted to the immigration authority.

13.3. Obligation of Employer to Enforce Immigration Laws

Employing, or arranging the employment of, an individual who is not authorized to work in Korea is a crime punishable by three years of imprisonment or a fine of up to KRW 30 million.[187] The fine may be applied to a corporate employer, as well as the individual responsible if the violation occurs under negligent supervision by the employer.[188]

Hiring foreign employees under the FWA, or employees with work-related visas, imposes reporting obligations on the employer with respect to things such as significant changes to employment terms and termination.[189]

Employers must purchase certain types of insurance coverage (or set up an equivalent trust) for the benefit of their foreign employees covered by the FWA, within fifteen days after they become employees.[190] Each of these employees must be covered by at least two types of insurance, Departure Guarantee Insurance and Wage Payment Guarantee Insurance, the purposes

184. FWA Enforcement Rule Art. 5-2, FWA Enforcement Decree Art. 13-4(2).
185. FWA Art. 18.
186. FWA Art. 18-2(1).
187. IA Art. 94(9)–(11).
188. IA Art. 99-3.
189. IA Art. 19, FWA Art. 17.
190. FWA Arts 13(1) & 23(1), FWA Enforcement Decree Arts 21(2) & 27(2).

of which are to secure each foreign employee's retirement/severance benefits and to insure against non-payment of wages, respectively.

Korea's primary labour laws, such as the LSA, apply to all employers and workplaces within Korean territory. Therefore, employers must generally protect foreign employees pursuant to these laws to the same extent as local employees.

Employers may not unfairly discriminate against foreign workers hired under the FWA, nor against any employees on the basis of nationality.[191] Where an FWA-covered employee returns home upon termination of employment, upon expiration of their permitted employment period, or due to any other reason, the employer must settle all payables and receivables, including wages, before the foreign employee departs Korea.[192]

13.4. Fines and Penalties

Hiring a foreign individual who is not authorized to work in Korea may be punished by imprisonment for up to three years, or by a fine not exceeding KRW 30 million. A person who employs a foreign worker without a required employment permit, or a person who has been punished due to a violation of the FWA or the IA, may be barred from employing foreign workers under the FWA for three years.[193,194]

Also, if an employer commits certain specified acts that are illegal under Korean labour law, the employer's FWA employment permit may be cancelled. In this event, the employer must terminate the employment contract with the relevant foreign employee within fifteen days from the date of cancellation of the permit.[195]

13.5. Secondment/Foreign Assignment

If a Korean employee is employed by a Korean employer in Korea and subsequently sent by the employer to work overseas, it is generally prudent to assume that Korean employment-law protections still apply while the employee works overseas. The MOEL long maintained the position that if a Korean employee is employed by a Korean employer in Korea, and subsequently sent by the employer to work overseas at the employer's

191. FWA Art. 22, LSA Art. 6.
192. FWA Art. 16.
193. FWA Art. 20(1).
194. Effective 11 Dec. 2022, the FWA was amended to punish employers by barring their ability to employ foreigners in the event that a violation of OSHA results in the death of a foreign worker. FWA Art. 20(1)(3-2).
195. FWA Art. 19(1)–(2).

workplace/affiliate in a foreign country, Korean employment-law protections would still apply while the employee works overseas. However, in December 2022, the MOEL abandoned its prior position and adopted a multi-factor test to determine the governing law for Korean employees assigned overseas. Identifying the governing law for employees assigned to work abroad can present complex issues and is somewhat controversial and unsettled. Korean labour law additionally protects all employees of any nationality whose main place of work is Korea.[196]

13.6. Checklist of Do's and Don'ts

- Korean labour law protects both foreign employees and Korean employees. Accordingly, employers must comply with Korean labour law with respect to foreigners employed in Korea.
- Employers must be careful not to hire unauthorized foreign workers, by checking the visa type and expiration date of all potential foreign employees.
- Bear in mind that Korean labour law is very likely to be applied to Korean employees hired by Korean employers in Korea and then sent or seconded to work abroad.

14. PROTECTION OF WHISTLE-BLOWING CLAIMS

14.1. Overview

Various acts protect particular whistle-blowing activities in Korea, but the most comprehensive whistleblower-protection law is the Protection of Public Interest Whistleblowers Act (the 'Whistleblowers Act'), which protects employees who report violations of the public interest. To protect their identity, whistleblowers can also report a whistle-blowing claim through an attorney. 'Violations of the public interest' include violations of an enumerated list of health and safety, consumer-protection, and fair-competition laws, and other statutes that protect the public interest. Employers are not permitted to impose any 'disadvantageous measures', including dismissal, on employees who report such violations. Employees who are treated disadvantageously for reporting such public interest violations may seek protective measures from the Anti-Corruption and Civil Rights Commission. The LSA is one of the laws subject to the Whistleblowers Act. Additionally, the LSA itself protects employees who report violations of its provisions. Article 104 of the LSA prohibits dismissal

196. Act on Private International Law Art. 48.

or other 'unfair treatment' of employees who report violations of the LSA to the MOEL or to a labour inspector. Additionally, any dismissal, demotion, pay cut, or other disadvantageous measure taken against an employee may be challenged by the employee for lack of just cause, and retaliation for whistle-blowing will not be considered just cause for any such measures. The Commission can impose an enforcement fine of up to KRW 30 million on employers who have not implemented protective measures by the due date. The Commission can repeatedly impose and collect the fine to compel compliance until protective measures are implemented, up to twice a year from the date on which a decision requiring protective measures is received.

14.2. Checklist of Do's and Don'ts

– Any disadvantageous measures taken against an employee, such as dismissal, demotion, or suspension, will in all cases need to be supported by just cause, for which the burden of proof lies with the employer. However, particular care should be taken in applying any such measures to employees who have reported potential legal violations to avoid running afoul of special whistleblower protections.

15. PROHIBITION OF DISCRIMINATION IN THE WORKPLACE

15.1. Overview of Anti-discrimination Laws

Article 11(1) of the Korean Constitution provides that 'all citizens shall not be discriminated against in all areas of his/her political, economic, social or cultural life on the basis of sex, religion or social status'. This principle of equal treatment and non-discrimination also applies to labour relationships. Article 32(4) of the Constitution more specifically stipulates that 'female workers shall be specially protected and shall not be unjustly discriminated against with respect to employment, wages and working conditions.'

The Framework Employment Policy Act (FEPA), the Employment Security Act (ESA), the TULRAA, and the National Human Rights Commission Act (NHRCA),[197] also provide various protections for employees prohibiting discrimination based on gender, religion, age, physical infirmities, social status, race, attended school, and national origin

197. A person who suffered a violation of human rights, including discriminatory acts, may file a petition with the National Human Rights Commission and the Commission may issue advice to rectify specific practices if they are deemed discriminatory. NHRCA Art. 30. However, the Commission's advice is not binding and it has no power to impose any penalty or to compel corrective action.

or hometown. However, some of these forms of prohibited discrimination lack any significant penalties or means of enforcement.[198] The more significant prohibitions of discriminatory conduct are discussed below.

In accordance with the general non-discrimination principle and the prohibition of discrimination against women under the Constitution, Article 6 of the LSA provides that any discriminatory treatment of employees on the basis of gender, nationality, religion, or social status is not permitted. The principle of anti-discrimination has become an even more important part of Korean labour law since the EEA was enacted in 1987.

Progressively, the scope of prohibited discrimination has expanded, and the protection of employees has been enhanced and diversified. Currently, no discrimination is permissible with regard to wages or other employment conditions; recruitment and employment; benefit plans; training, placement and promotion; retirement age; resignation and dismissal; transfers; employment support service; provision of employment information; and training for occupational capacity development and job-placement support.

15.2. Age Discrimination

The AEPA prohibits discrimination on the basis of age without justifiable reasons in all labour-related areas such as recruitment, employment, wages, education/training, placement, transfer, promotion, dismissal, and retirement.[199] The AEPA's prohibition of discrimination specifically includes conduct and policies that have a disparate impact on different age groups.[200]

An employee who has suffered from a discriminatory act based on age may file a petition with the National Human Rights Commission pursuant to Article 30 of the NHRCA. The Commission may then issue non-binding advice and will notify the MOEL thereof. If the employer fails to comply with the Commission's resulting advice without providing any justifiable reason, and if the discrimination is substantial, the MOEL, either at the employee's request or sua sponte, may order the employer to rectify the discriminatory behaviour.[201] Failure to comply with such an order may result in an administrative fine of up to KRW 30 million. In addition, discriminatory treatment in the context of recruiting or hiring may be subject

198. For example, the FEPA and the ESA provide no mechanism for enforcement nor any penalty for violations. Thus, for example, the FEPA's prohibition on discrimination in recruiting based on an applicant's attended school or level of education, is less significant than other forms of prohibited discrimination that have a clear mechanism for enforcement.

199. AEPA Art. 4-4.

200. AEPA Art. 4-4(2).

201. AEPA Arts 4-7.

to a fine of up to KRW 5 million, separately from the petition process through the National Human Rights Commission.[202]

The AEPA also prohibits retaliation against an employee for filing any petition, suit, or report regarding age discrimination prohibited by the AEPA, with a potential penalty of up to two years of imprisonment or by a fine of up to KRW 10 million.[203]

Imposing a mandatory retirement age on employees is not considered discrimination on the basis of age, if done in accordance with the law.[204] The AEPA requires that the mandatory retirement age be 60 or above.[205]

Recently, there has been significant debate over whether so-called 'wage-peak' systems, under which employees' wages gradually decrease after a certain age, violate the AEPA. On 26 May 2022, the Supreme Court decided a landmark case in which the Court found that a certain employer's wage-peak system constituted illegal age discrimination in violation of the AEPA.[206] The Court laid out several factors a court should examine to determine whether there exists a 'justifiable' reason to discriminate on the basis of age in the form of a wage-peak system, including: (i) whether the purpose of introducing the wage-peak system is justifiable; (ii) the degree of negative impact on the affected employees; (iii) whether any counterbalancing measures that can justify the wage cut have been taken and their appropriateness; and (iv) whether the savings from establishing the wage-peak system have actually been used for the originally intended purpose. It remains to be settled how these factors will apply to other companies' wage-peak systems. One circumstance that distinguishes this case is that the employer's establishment of a wage-peak system was unrelated to any increase in the company's retirement age, whereas many companies which have implemented wage-peak systems did so to counterbalance the impact of having to increase their mandatory retirement ages after the relevant law was amended to raise the minimum mandatory retirement age to 60.

15.3. Race Discrimination

Other than as specifically prohibited under the TULRAA,[207] there is no particular statute that punishes racial discrimination. However, the general complaint procedure for discrimination claims under the NHRCA, which

202. AEPA Arts 23-3(2).
203. AEPA Arts 4-9, 23-3(1).
204. AEPA Art. 4-5(3).
205. AEPA Art. 19.
206. S. Ct. Case No. 2017Da292343 (26 May 2022).
207. TULRAA Art. 9.

may result in non-binding recommendations, applies to racial discrimination.

15.4. Sex Discrimination/Sexual Harassment

The LSA prohibits discriminatory acts against employees based on gender.[208] Discriminatory acts include unfavourable treatment of female employees without any justifiable non-discriminatory reason. An employer that violates this provision may be punished by a fine not exceeding KRW 5 million.

The EEA also prohibits discrimination based on gender with respect to employees, and also with respect to potential employees, as to whom it bans gender-based discrimination in recruitment and hiring. Employers that discriminate on the basis of gender with respect to their retirement age, or with respect to resignation and dismissal, are subject to imprisonment for not more than five years or a fine not exceeding KRW 30 million. Discrimination on the basis of gender in wages is punishable by imprisonment for up to three years or a fine not exceeding KRW 30 million.[209] Finally, other gender-based discrimination not falling under the aforementioned categories, including with respect to hiring or recruiting, is punishable by a fine not exceeding KRW 5 million.[210] The EEA generally includes acts and policies that have a disparate impact on men and women, within its definition of discriminatory acts, but excludes discrimination where: (i) a specific gender is required in the light of the nature of the job duties; (ii) measures are taken to protect maternity; and (iii) affirmative action measures are taken in accordance with the EEA or other laws.[211]

Sexual harassment in the workplace is strictly prohibited under the EEA.[212] Sexual harassment in the workplace typically involves a situation where an employer (including a person in a supervisory position or a co-worker), using his/her position at work or in relation to work, makes an employee feel sexually humiliated or offended by using sexual language or behaviour or giving disadvantageous treatment in employment matters based on the rejection of sexual approaches or requests. Whether sexual harassment has taken place is determined based on the reasonable perception of the complaining party regardless of the subjective intent of the alleged harasser.

208. LSA Art. 6.
209. EEA Art. 37(2).
210. EEA Art. 37(4).
211. EEA Art. 2.
212. EEA Art. 12.

Employers are responsible for ensuring that the workplace is free from sexual harassment. Employers are required to educate employees on the prevention of sexual harassment in the workplace by providing training sessions, holding meetings, offering internet training, or other means, at least once a year.[213] When a claim of sexual harassment is substantiated, an employer must take disciplinary or other appropriate actions. Failure to take such action may result in an administrative fine of up to KRW 5 million.[214] Additionally, the victim of sexual harassment may report it to the local office of the MOEL, and/or file a petition with the National Human Rights Commission. Under the Civil Act, the victim has a right to demand compensation from both the individual and the employer for damages resulting from their illegal acts. Aggravated sexual harassment may also be subject to criminal punishment.

If an employee complains of sexual harassment by a work-related third party, including vendors or customers, the employer is legally obliged to take all appropriate measures, such as relocation of the complaining employee.[215]

Under the EEA, an employer that takes adverse measures against an employee who has been a victim of sexual harassment in the workplace or who has claimed or reported an occurrence of sexual harassment may be punished by imprisonment of up to three years or by a fine of up to KRW 30 million.[216] The EEA also now imposes an affirmative duty to investigate allegations of sexual harassment without delay.[217] It requires the employer to take protective measures to shield the victim claiming sexual harassment both during the investigation and after.[218] It requires that the victim's opinions be considered before imposing disciplinary action on a harasser.[219] And it imposes express confidentiality obligations on the people involved in the investigation, preventing disclosure of confidential information without the victim's consent.[220] Violation of these requirements is subject to an administrative fine of up to KRW 5 million.[221]

The obligation to provide sexual-harassment-prevention training is a statutory obligation, rather than merely a regulation,[222] and a penalty of up

---

213. EEA Art. 13, EEA Enforcement Decree Art. 3. An employer with fewer than ten employees can satisfy the anti-sexual-harassment training obligation simply by providing appropriate materials.
214. EEA Art. 39(3)(1-6).
215. EEA Art. 14-2(1).
216. EEA Art. 37(2)(2).
217. EEA Art. 14(2).
218. EEA Art. 14(2)–(4).
219. EEA Art. 14(5).
220. EEA Art. 14(7).
221. EEA Art. 39(3)(1-7).
222. EEA Art. 13(1).

to KRW 5 million may be imposed for non-compliance.[223] Employers are required to make sexual-harassment-prevention materials available and known to employees in an accessible place,[224] subject to a penalty of up to KRW 5 million.[225] And employers are required to take measures to prevent and prohibit sexual harassment in the workplace in accordance with standards prescribed by the MOEL.

The LSA requires most companies to address non-sexual workplace harassment in their Rules of Employment and imposes various obligations regarding how to respond to allegations of non-sexual workplace harassment. The LSA imposes penalties for retaliation against a victim or other employee reporting non-sexual workplace harassment: imprisonment for up to three years or a fine of up to KRW 30 million.[226] And if one fails to adequately reflect the new anti-harassment law in one's rules of employment, there can be corrective orders and, eventually, fines imposed.

Additional administrative penalties regarding non-sexual workplace harassment became effective on 14 October 2021. First, an administrative fine of up to KRW 10 million now applies to an employer (or certain family members of an employer) who commits workplace harassment. Second, an administrative fine of up to KRW 5 million now applies to (i) an employer who does not immediately commence an investigation after receiving a report or gaining knowledge of workplace harassment; (ii) an employer who, after confirming the occurrence of workplace harassment through such investigation, fails to take adequate protective measures for the victim, upon the victim's request; (iii) an employer who, after confirming the occurrence of workplace harassment through such investigation, fails to take adequate measures regarding the harasser, or takes such measures without soliciting the victim's opinion; and (iv) anyone who was involved in the investigation and leaked any confidential information gained through such investigation, against the victim's will.[227]

As of 19 May 2022, employees are able to file a petition with the Labor Relations Commission against their employer for gender discrimination (gender discrimination includes discrimination with respect to wages, promotion, recruitment, etc.), sexual harassment, or failure to take certain measures in response to reports of sexual harassment, and the available remedies include damages.[228] Compensation for an employee victim has previously only been available via civil lawsuit. If the Labor Relations Commission finds that gender discrimination in employment occurred, it may issue a corrective order and require the employer to pay compensation

223. EEA Art. 39(3)(1-2).
224. EEA Art. 13(3).
225. EEA Art. 39(3)(1-3).
226. LSA Art. 109(1).
227. LSA Art. 116(2).
228. EEA Arts 26–29.

of up to three times the actual damages of the employee.[229] Any such corrective order may also be applied to other employees who have been discriminated against. The Labor Relations Commission will also be empowered to issue corrective orders and award up to treble damages where an employer has failed to take required measures with respect to a sexual-harassment victim or harasser, or in the case of any retaliation.

15.5. Handicap and Disability Discrimination

The PDA prohibits employers from engaging in any discriminatory practices against people with disabilities with respect to recruitment, employment, wages and benefit plans, education, placement, promotion, transfer, retirement age, and resignation or dismissal.[230] In addition, the PDA provides that labour unions shall neither reject admission of any worker with a disability into a union nor discriminate against disabled workers in regard to any rights and activities as a member.[231] Discrimination includes acts that have a disparate impact on disabled people without reasonable grounds.[232]

If a person commits a discriminatory act prohibited under the PDA, and such act is deemed to be malicious, a court may sentence the discriminator to imprisonment for not more than three years or a fine not exceeding KRW 30 million. For this purpose, malice is determined after considering the wilfulness, continuousness, and repetition of the discriminatory act or acts and other circumstances. Notwithstanding the penalties above, a person who suffered harm due to a discriminatory act may file a petition with the National Human Rights Commission, which may issue recommendations that can be acted on by the Ministry of Justice, in a manner similar to that by which the MOEL handles complaints of age discrimination discussed above.

The PDA mandates employers that regularly employ at least thirty employees to provide enumerated kinds of reasonable accommodation for people with disabilities (including structural changes or working hours' accommodation) to allow them to work under equitable working conditions with non-disabled employees. The rejection of a request for accommodation may constitute unlawful discrimination.[233]

Additionally, under the Employment Promotion and Vocational Rehabilitation for Disabled Persons Act (EPRDPA), employers with fifty or more employees are required to hire disabled persons so that they comprise

229. EEA Art. 29-2(2).
230. PDA Art. 10(1).
231. PDA Art. 10(2).
232. PDA Art. 4(1)(2).
233. PDA Art. 11.

a certain percentage of their workforce (currently 3.1% as of 1 January 2023 for private companies and 3.6% for public companies). Employers may be required by the MOEL to submit a plan for employing the required ratio of disabled employees and to report their progress, and employers may be fined for failing to submit the required plans or reports.[234] And if an employer ordinarily has one hundred or more employees, it must pay a fee to the government for each disabled person that it is required to hire but fails to do so, with the per capita fee increasing based on the magnitude of the shortfall.[235] A similar hiring mandate with a workforce ratio of between 3% and 8% (depending on industry) applies to certain categories of veterans and their immediate family members,[236] but the potential penalties for non-compliance are less substantial because they do not include a per capita fee.

15.6. National Origin Discrimination

The LSA prohibits an employer from discriminating against employees on the basis of their nationality.[237] A violation of this provision is subject to a fine not exceeding KRW 5 million.

The FWA also provides that an employer shall not unfairly treat or discriminate against an employee on the grounds of being a foreign worker.[238] However, there is no penalty specified for a violation.

15.7. Religious Discrimination

The LSA prohibits discriminatory acts against workers on the basis of their religion[239] and provides that any employer who fails to comply with this provision may be punished by a fine not exceeding KRW 5 million. Although there are no controlling court precedents, the prevailing view is that accommodation of employees' religious practices is not legally required.

234. EPRDPA Art. 28, EPRDPA Enforcement Decree Arts 25 & 27.
235. EPRDPA Art. 33.
236. Act on the Honorable Treatment of and Support for Persons of Distinguished Service to the State Art. 33-2.
237. LSA Art. 6.
238. FWA Art. 22.
239. LSA Art. 6.

15.8. Pregnancy Discrimination

Under the EEA, pregnancy is included within the definition of prohibited gender-based discrimination.[240] Accordingly, an employer may not discriminate against female employees or potential employees on the basis of pregnancy, in virtually all employment-related areas such as wages, benefit plans, education/placement, promotion, retirement age, and resignation or dismissal. Any pregnancy discrimination in recruitment and employment, pecuniary benefits other than wages, education, placement, or promotion shall be punished by a fine not exceeding KRW 5 million. Any discrimination on the basis of pregnancy in wages is subject to imprisonment for not more than three years or a fine not exceeding KRW 30 million, whereas discrimination on the basis of pregnancy in retirement age, resignation, and dismissal is subject to imprisonment for not more than five years or a fine not exceeding KRW 30 million.

Also, discrimination in providing maternity leave, and childcare and family-care leave and reduced hours is prohibited. Specifically, an employer is prohibited from firing or applying unfavourable treatment based on an employee requesting or using such leave or reduced hours. Violations are subject to criminal penalties of up to three years of imprisonment or a fine of up to KRW 30 million.

An employer is also prohibited from firing or applying unfavourable treatment to, an employee during a childcare leave period except where the business itself cannot continue. Firing, or applying unfavourable treatment, to an employee on the grounds of taking reduced hours for childcare is also prohibited. Pro rata pay reduction or other legitimate measures to reflect the reduced working hours are permissible, however.[241] Violations are subject to criminal penalties of up to three years of imprisonment or a fine of up to KRW 30 million.

15.9. Marital Status Discrimination

Article 11 of the EEA provides that an employer may not enter into an employment contract that requires a female employee to resign upon her marriage. The purpose of this Article is to rectify a custom by which female employees were expected and required to quit their jobs upon marriage. Any employer who violates this prohibition may be punished by imprisonment for not more than five years or by a fine not exceeding KRW 30 million. In

240. EEA Art. 2(1).

241. EEA Art. 19-3(1). However, although a pro rata pay reduction to reflect actual hours worked is allowed with respect to a period of reduced hours for childcare under the EEA, it is not permitted with respect to reduced working hours during pregnancy under the LSA.

this case, the law specifies only 'female employees', but whether an employee is male or female, an employment contract demanding resignation on the grounds of marriage is null and void.

15.10. Sexual Orientation Discrimination

Any discrimination based on sexual orientation is prohibited under the NHRCA, and the National Human Rights Commission may investigate any complaint. Upon finding any violation, the Commission may provide advice for its correction.

15.11. Retaliation

In addition to other statutory prohibitions on retaliation – of which some significant ones are mentioned above – if any employer dismisses or treats an employee unfavourably for reporting the employer's violation of the LSA, such as for discriminating against an employer based on the nationality, religious belief, religion, or social status, the employer may be punished by imprisonment for not more than two years or by a fine not exceeding KRW 10 million.

Even in the absence of any specific prohibition of retaliation, any dismissal, disciplinary action, or unfavourable treatment of an employee on the grounds of having reported discriminatory treatment or having filed a lawsuit with respect to discriminatory treatment, is prohibited because it does not constitute 'just cause' under Article 23 of the LSA.

15.12. Constructive Discharge

Korean jurisprudence does not have an explicit concept of 'constructive dismissal'. But an employee may allege, in a wrongful termination suit before the Labor Relations Commission or court, that an ostensibly voluntary dismissal was, in fact, involuntary – and thus required just cause under Article 23 of the LSA – because it was procured through coercive means.

15.13. Checklist of Do's and Don'ts

- Be well-acquainted with the anti-discrimination rules set forth in various acts and regulations.

- Note that discriminatory dismissal or unfavourable treatment is subject to specific penalties set forth by the relevant laws. Moreover, the foregoing can also be treated as unfair dismissal or unfair employment action. Therefore, a worker may bring a lawsuit or file a request for a remedy with the Labor Relations Commission.
- Be aware that it is mandatory to provide preventive education regarding sexual harassment at least once a year. Records must be preserved (*see* section 9.9), and compliance is subject to regular audit by the MOEL.

16. PRIVACY, TECHNOLOGY AND TRANSFER OF PERSONAL DATA

16.1. Privacy Rights of Employees

16.1.1. Grounds of Privacy Rights for Employees

The Korean Constitution does not contain any express obligation to protect personal information. However, Article 17 of the Constitution expresses a general right to privacy and Article 10 of the Constitution guarantees citizens' human worth and dignity, and their right to pursue happiness. The Constitutional Court has also recognized the right of self-determination over personal information as an independent basic right under the Constitution.[242]

In addition, the primary statute that generally regulates the treatment of personal information is the Personal Information Protection Act (PIPA), which came into force on 30 September 2011. The 'Act on the Promotion of Information and Communications Network Utilization and Information Protection' (Network Act) also has provisions governing privacy rights connected with the use of online networks, but most of these rights and obligations were subsumed into PIPA effective as of 5 August 2020. Personal location information is specially regulated by the 'Act on the Protection, Use, etc., of Location Information' (Location Information Act).

However, special regulations regarding personal information under the LSA, the EIA, and the OSHA take precedence where an employer collects or uses the personal information of employees.

Employers are required by law to keep records of a variety of information and preserve various kinds of documentation, relating to their employees, as discussed in section 9.9. Employers may also keep additional, non-mandatory information about their employees, provided they obtain employees' consent. These employee records and documentation will comprise or contain 'personal information' protected by Korean privacy law, as discussed below.

242. Constitutional Court Case Nos 99Ma513 and 2004Ma190, 26 May 2005.

The personal information of employees that is gathered and used by their employer is protected in accordance with the right of self-determination over personal information under the Constitution, PIPA, and the Location Information Act. Additionally, under Korean law, employees also have limited privacy rights respecting the information that they store on company property, such as computer hard drives or servers. For example, it is not permitted to freely inspect an employee's computer files or emails, even if stored on company-owned computer systems, without consent or sufficient justification; even if an unqualified right to do so is provided for in an employment contract or in the company's rules of employment, such an unqualified right is not enforceable.

16.1.2. Definition of 'Personal Information'

According to Article 2 of PIPA, the term 'personal information' refers to any information that pertains to a living person, including the person's full name, resident registration number, images, and other information, which can, by itself or easily combined with other information, identify the person.

16.1.3. Collection and Use of Employee Personal Information

General Principles

In general, an employer must obtain an individual's consent in order to collect personal information about that individual, including employees or potential employees. When obtaining such consent, the employer must notify the individual, in advance, of the purposes of collecting and using the personal information, the items of personal information to be collected, and the period for which personal information will be retained and used, as well as the individual's right to withhold consent and the details of any disadvantage that will result from the individual's refusal to consent.[243] This information – and other enumerated items of information – is also required to be covered generally by the employer's privacy policy, which must be established and made available to employees through the employer's website, or other permissible means.[244]

However, an employer is permitted to collect and use the personal information of job applicants or employees without their consent: (1) if permitted by another statute or if required in order to perform statutory obligations; (2) if required for executing and implementing a contract (such

243. PIPA Art. 15.

244. PIPA Art. 30, PIPA Enforcement Decree Art. 31.

as the work experience, qualifications, educational background, supporting documents, and contact information of job applicants); (3) if clearly required for the imminent protection of the life, health, or property interests of the subject individual or a third party, where advance consent cannot be obtained due to incapacity, unknown address, or other similar reasons; and (4) if necessary to protect the employer's legitimate interests that clearly outweigh the subject's rights, to the extent that the information collected is sufficiently relevant and limited to a reasonable scope.

Statutory obligations that justify the collection and use of personal information include, for example, the requisite preparation of an employee registry and wage ledger required under the LSA; the preservation of the reported results of mandatory medical examinations; and information required for employees' year-end tax adjustment, which includes personal information of both employees and their family members.[245]

Whenever an employer collects or uses the personal information of job applicants or employees, the employer must collect and use only the minimally required personal information for the purpose, and must separately classify and collect required information (for which consent is not required for use) and optional information (for which consent is required for use).[246]

If an employer collects personal information from third parties, the employer is additionally required to notify the individual of the source, the purpose, and the individual's right to disallow the employer's collection and use of the information, either at the applicant's request or if the employer processes a significant amount of personal information (set by regulation).[247]

Further Restrictions on Handling Unique Identifying Information and Sensitive Information

There are additional restrictions on handling both unique identifying information and sensitive information. Unique identifying information includes an individual's resident registration number, driver's license number, passport number, and alien registration number. Sensitive information refers to any information such as an individual's thoughts, beliefs, entry into or withdrawal from a labour union or political party, political opinions, health, sex life, genetic information, and criminal history. Unique identifying information and sensitive information cannot be collected or used except as provided in another statute, or after obtaining the

245. Income Tax Act (ITA) Art. 140, ITA Enforcement Decree Arts 106, 108, 113 and 114, ITA Enforcement Regulation Art. 58 and Form No. 37.
246. PIPA Arts 16 & 22.
247. PIPA Art. 20.

individual's consent separately from any more general consent to the collection of personal information.[248]

Resident registration numbers may be collected or used only where handling the resident registration number is: (1) specifically required or permitted by law, (2) required for the imminent protection of the life, health, or property interests of the subject of the registration number or a third party, or (3) as otherwise determined by the Personal Information Protection Committee. Virtually all employers are, however, required to collect and use their employees' resident registration numbers for a number of purposes under various labour-related statutes such as the LSA, the EIA, and the ITA. But an employer should not collect an individual's resident registration number until after having hired that individual.

16.1.4. Provision of Personal Information to Third Parties and Management of Personal Information by Third Parties

In order to provide an employee's personal information to a third party, an employer must generally obtain written consent from the employee. To obtain an employee's consent, the employer must notify the employee in advance of: (1) the recipient of the information; (2) the recipient's purpose for using the personal information; (3) the items of personal information to be provided; (4) the period for which the recipient will retain and use the personal information; and (5) the employee's right not to consent, and the details of any disadvantage that will result from such refusal.[249]

However, the employee's personal information can be provided to a third party without the consent of the employee if: (i) it is authorized by statute or required in order to perform a statutory obligation; or (ii) the prior consent of the employee or the employee's legal representative cannot be obtained, and it is clearly necessary for the imminent protection of the life, health, or property interests of the employee or a third party.[250]

An employer that intends to entrust a third party with handling its employees' personal information (i.e., for purposes of administering year-end tax adjustments, job-application forms, or pension plans) must do so by means of a writing covering specific matters enumerated in PIPA and its associated regulations, including restrictions on the scope of use and on further third-party transfers, and specification of the means by which the information will be protected.[251] And the employer must disclose to the subject employees the particular information entrusted to the third party and

248. PIPA Art. 17.
249. PIPA Arts 23 & 24.
250. PIPA Art. 18(2).
251. PIPA Art. 26(1).

the identity of the third-party trustee; this disclosure must be made in a manner that enables the employees to easily access the information, through means prescribed by regulation (such as the employer's website).[252]

On 10 November 2022, the Supreme Court held that reporting a crime to the police can be a violation of PIPA if the criminal filings include documents that contain personal identifying information, such as security footage, names, addresses and bank account numbers.[253] The Supreme Court's decision recognized that submitting materials for a prosecution and reporting a crime may also be considered a disclosure of personal information.

16.1.5. Administrative, Technical, and Physical Information and Data Protection Measures

In order to protect employees' personal information, an employer must take a variety of administrative measures (such as establishment and implementation of internal controls and restrictions on access, and appointment of a privacy officer); technical measures (such as maintenance of an access control system, use of encryption, maintenance of reliable access records, installation of security programmes); and physical security measures, according to the standards enumerated by regulation under PIPA.[254]

Employers are required to take various measures to notify affected individuals and mitigate the harm from any data breach or leak of personal information. An employer may be held liable for any damage resulting from a data breach or other information leak unless the employer can prove it was neither wilful nor negligent.[255]

16.1.6. Destruction of Personal Information

Personal information that is no longer necessary upon achievement of the purpose for which the personal information was obtained and used or for other reasons, or upon expiration of the retention period, shall be destroyed without delay in a manner that prevents the relevant information from being restored or reproduced unless it is required to be preserved by law.[256]

252. PIPA Art. 26(2).
253. S. Ct. Case No. 2018Do1966 (10 Nov. 2022). The case involved a director of a cooperative reporting a crime pertaining to the president of the cooperative.
254. PIPA Arts 29–31, PIPA Enforcement Decree Arts 30–32.
255. PIPA Art. 39.
256. PIPA Art. 21.

Thus, when an employee leaves the employer's service, personal information that is not required to be preserved must be destroyed without delay. In order to keep information longer than the period required by applicable law (most commonly three years for employment-related information; *see* section 9.9), an employer must obtain the employee's consent.

16.1.7. Employee Access Rights to Personnel Records

Employees have a range of rights to the inspection, correction, and deletion of their personal information maintained by their employer.

Employees may request their employer to permit access to their personal information and to correct, delete, or cease handling their information. In response, the employer must take proper measures unless there is a justifiable reason to deny the request, such as the information being required for the performance of statutory obligations. However, if the access is prohibited by law, likely to harm the life or health of third parties, or likely to unfairly infringe on the property or other interests of third parties, the employer may restrict such access or deny such request after notifying the relevant employee of the reasons.[257]

After accessing their personal information, employees may request that their employer correct it, or delete it unless the relevant information is required to be kept by law. Unless any special procedure to correct or delete personal information is prescribed by law, the employer must immediately inspect the information and take appropriate measures pursuant to the request, such as correction or deletion, and then inform the employee of the result.[258]

Employees may request the employer to cease handling some or all of their personal information. The employer may deny the request only where: (i) there is a specific legal requirement or authorization to keep the information; (ii) it is required in order to perform obligations imposed by law; (iii) it is required to perform obligations under the relevant contract and no clear intent to terminate the contract was expressed; or (iv) doing so is likely to physically harm a third party or to unduly infringe the interests of a third party.[259]

Personal information access rights continue after an employee leaves the employer's service. Thus, an employer must allow access and the opportunity to correct or request deletion of incorrect personal information

257. PIPA Art. 35.
258. PIPA Art. 36.
259. PIPA Art. 37.

to former employees while such records are retained unless relevant exceptions apply.

16.2. Checklist of Do's and Don'ts

- Violation of employees' rights with respect to their personal information can result in criminal penalties as well as potential civil damages, so attention to the law's requirements is of great importance.
- When hiring employees, an employer must collect certain required personal information from job applicants. In general, a job applicant's name, telephone number, address, educational background, grades, experience and qualifications (if the applicant's educational background, work experience, and qualifications are required for the performance of the relevant job duties) are considered to be the minimally required personal information collected in the hiring process.
- Generally, an employer should collect personal information directly from the job applicants. If the employer collects personal information from third parties, the employer must notify the applicant of the source, the purpose, and the information collected, and the applicant's right to disallow the employer's collection and use of the information.
- In order to maintain and use the personal information of job applicants who are not ultimately hired, the employer must identify the retention period and obtain consent from the individuals to which the information pertains.
- In order to prepare the list of employees and the payroll required by the LSA, an employer may collect and use an employee's name, gender, date of birth, resident registration number, address, work experience, start date of the employment or contract renewal, period of contract, wage information, and other required details without the employee's consent.
- An employer may collect and use personal information about its employees' family members in order to provide welfare benefits and process the employee's yearly tax adjustment, without the consent of the family members.
- An employer may also use employees' health-related information for the purpose of fulfilling its responsibility for protecting and maintaining the employee's health without their consent.
- An employer is not only potentially liable for its own data breaches but can be held liable for any infringement of employees' rights respecting their personal information by a third party that is entrusted with the handling of their personal information. If employees' rights respecting their personal information are infringed by the third-party trustee's illegal

acts, the employer may also be liable for damages incurred by such infringement.

17. REQUIRED NOTICES AND POSTINGS

17.1. Overview

Employers subject to the MWA must post a notice or otherwise appropriately notify employees of the minimum wage rate applicable to them, the wages that are included in calculating the minimum wage, the scope of any excluded employees, and the effective date. This notification must be made one day prior to the effective date of the minimum wage.[260]

The major aspects of the LSA and its Enforcement Decree must also be posted or made available in the workplace of an employer with five or more employees.[261]

The company's privacy policy must be made available, as discussed in section 16.

And the major requirements of the OSHA must be posted or made available at the workplace.[262] Also, employers who are not exempt from the requirement because of their size and nature must create and post or make available their health-and-safety regulations at the workplace.

260. MWA Art. 11, MWA Enforcement Decree Art. 11.
261. LSA Art. 14, LSA Enforcement Decree Art. 7 & Table 1.
262. OSHA Art. 34.

www.ingramcontent.com/pod-product-compliance
Lightning Source LLC
Chambersburg PA
CBHW071354230926
51846CB00002B/557
9789403521671